SPIES, CODE BREAKERS, AND SECRET AGENTS

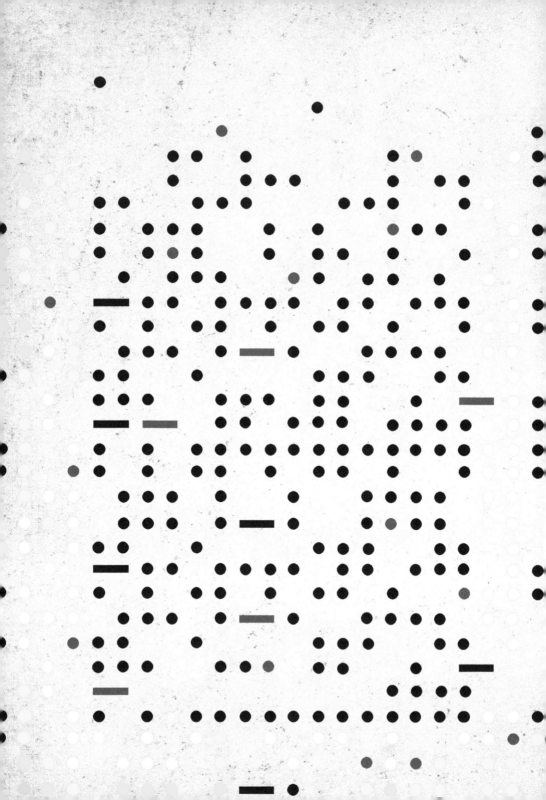

SPIES, CODE BREAKERS, AND SECRET AGENTS

A WORLD WAR II BOOK FOR KIDS

—— WRITTEN BY ——
CAROLE P. ROMAN

—— ILLUSTRATED BY ——
ALESSANDRA SANTELLI

ROCKRIDGE
PRESS

Cover and Interior Designer: Angela Navarra

Photo Art Director/Art Manager: Sara Feinstein

Editor: Kristen Depken

Developmental Editor: Lisa Trusiani

Production Editor: Chris Gage

Illustrations: Alessandra Santelli

ISBN: Print 978-1-64611-101-5 | eBook 978-1-64611-102-2

R1

For my family.

"All gave some, some gave all."

—

**HOWARD
WILLIAM
OSTERKAMP**

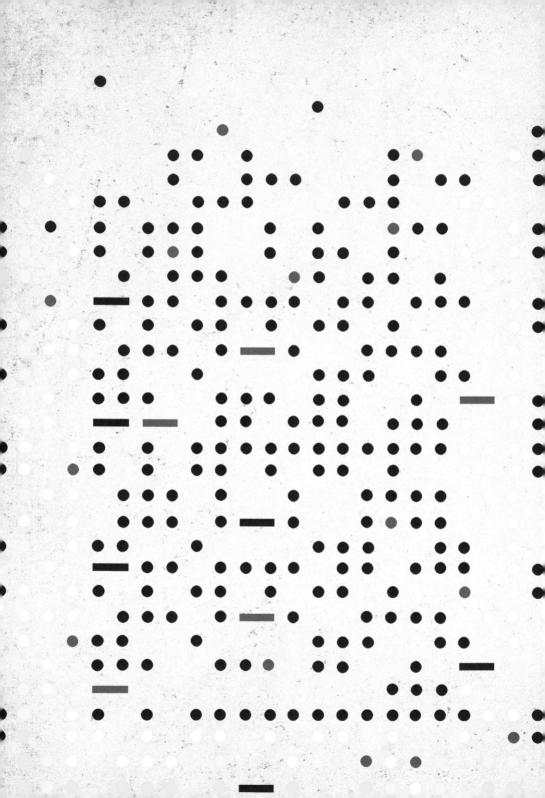

CONTENTs

INTRODUCTION • • • X

CHAPTER 1: SPIES ALL AROUND • • • 1

CHAPTER 2: SPY MISSIONS • • • 19

CHAPTER 3: SPY GEAR • • • 38

CHAPTER 4: SECRET ARMIES • • • 56

CHAPTER 5: SUPER SPIES • • • 66

CHAPTER 6: CODE BREAKERS • • • 104

CONCLUSION: SPIES TODAY • • • 115

GLOSSARY • • • 118

RESOURCES • • • 124

BIBLIOGRAPHY • • • 127

INDEX • • • 132

■	Axis powers, 1942
■	Countries controlled by Axis powers, 1942
■	Allied territory, 1942
■	Neutral countries, 1942
✳	Major battle

SW

NORWAY

DENMARK

B

GE

UNITED
KINGDOM

IRELAND

London
Dunkirk
BELGIUM
Normandy
Paris
FRANCE

NETH.

LUX.

SWITZ.

ITALY

Vichy
VICHY
(France)

PORTUGAL

SPAIN

Rom

Salern

Palerm

Spanish
Morocco

Oran

Algiers

Tunis

Casablanca

Morocco
(France)

Algeria
(France)

Tunisia
(France)

FINLAND
N
W
E
S
Leningrad
Moscow
SOVIET UNION
Stalingrad
Kursk
Warsaw
OVAKIA
ROMANIA
Budapest
NGARY
Yalta
ATIA
SERBIA
MONT.
BULGARIA
ALB.
TURKEY
GREECE
Syria (France)
IRA
Lebanon (France)
Palestine (Britain)
Transjorda
(Britain)
El Alamein
Tobruk
Cairo
SAUD

INTRODUCTION

From September 1939 to the final days of 1945, countries chose sides and an earth-shattering war took place between two giants—the **Allied Forces** and the **Axis Powers**. It was World War II.

The major Allied Forces were Great Britain, France, the United States, and the **Soviet Union**, while the major Axis Powers were **Nazi** Germany, Italy, and Japan.

Victories were great and small, and both sides used a secret weapon—spies—to help win battles. Spies helped the Allies win some of their greatest victories and eventually the war.

Spies worked in secret. They collected information about the enemy and reported it to the agent or agencies that handled them. The right information helped the military understand what the enemy was planning.

Spies existed in the shadows; their lives were in constant danger. Some lived with the enemy, pretending to be someone else. A careless word or gesture could lead to arrest, torture, and execution.

Their work was secret, so spies rarely received attention or awards. We know some of their identities, but there are many we will never know.

This book is about the role of **intelligence** agencies and spies in World War II. It starts with a brief overview of the war. Then it covers the places spies worked in the world and their top secret missions, as well as the creative gear they used to do their dangerous work. It introduces spy agencies—the organizations that **recruited** and trained spies, then sent them on their missions. It reveals the identities of World War II's most famous spies, as well as double agents and code breakers.

In each chapter, there are two different kinds of sidebars. One sidebar uses numbers to highlight an aspect of **espionage**. The other sidebar presents a fascinating fact. The book ends by exploring the role of spies in the world today.

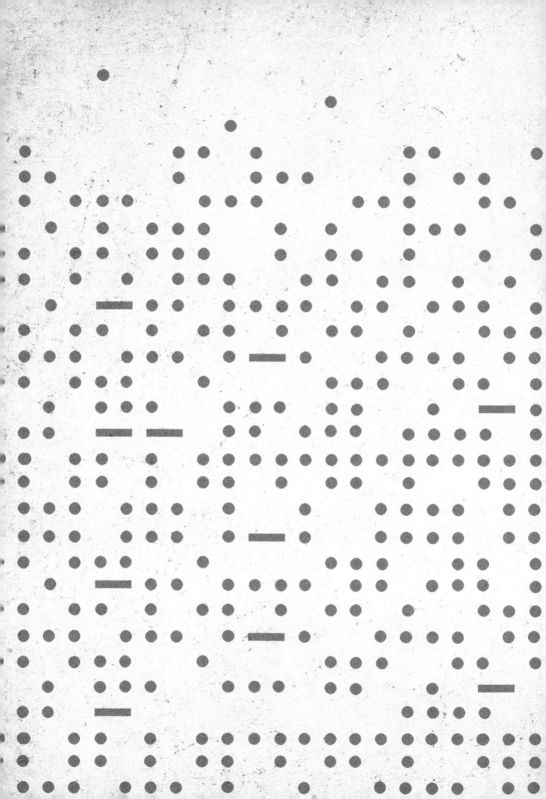

CHAPTER 1

SPIES ALL AROUND

SPIES PLAYED AN IMPORTANT PART in the war effort. Without their courage and willingness to put themselves in danger, the Allied Forces would not have won the war.

During World War II, almost every country created spy organizations or recruited more spies for the agencies it already had. Spies, or secret **agents**, were sent to live in foreign countries with the enemy. Spies gathered information and led **intrigue** that would help keep their own country safe, weaken the enemy, or win battles. For every spy that Germany sent to foreign countries during World War II, the Allies had agents on secret missions, too.

• • WORLD WAR II BEGINS WITH WORLD WAR I • •

Before there was World War II, there was World War I. It lasted from 1914 to 1918. World War I ended when Great Britain, France, Russia, and the United States, which were members of the Allied Powers, defeated Germany. Both sides signed a peace agreement, the **Treaty of Versailles**.

While all people were saddened and angry about the great loss of life and the destruction of their lands, Germany was also bitter about the treaty. Germany had to give payments, called **reparations**, to France. The money was for repairing roads, bridges, and buildings destroyed or damaged in the war.

To make these payments, Germany had to tax its people. An economic depression had spread around the world, but it hit Germany especially hard. Many German people starved.

Germany was a democracy, but these money problems made the government unstable. Adolf Hitler became the leader of the German people. His Nazi party was **fascist**, not democratic. The Nazis rose to power and Hitler became a dictator. Hitler had plans to march the

German military across Europe, invading countries along the way. Hitler began to make deals to ensure no one would try to stop him. It set the stage for World War II.

•• WORLD WAR II IN EUROPE ••

Hitler was ruthless and power-hungry. He wanted to invade neighboring countries and steal their resources. If Germany could take another country's oil and minerals, and force its citizens to work as slaves or fight for the Germans, then Germany could rebuild its military and become powerful again.

Hitler didn't want to fight the Soviets. He made them an offer: Germany would never invade the Soviet Union if the Soviet Union let Germany invade Poland. The Soviets agreed.

The deal between Germany and the Soviet Union alarmed France and Britain. If Hitler went into Poland and the Soviets didn't stop him, the German military would get stronger and could invade more countries. Perhaps Germany would attack France, as it had in World War I. Britain and France had a strong friendship with Poland. Both countries promised they would support Poland if Germany invaded.

By 1939, Germany's expansion had begun. Nazi German rule had already been welcomed in Austria, and Germany had also taken over areas of Czechoslovakia. When Germany invaded Poland, the Soviet Union kept its promise to Germany. It did nothing to help its neighbor Poland. France and Britain declared war on Germany within days, but they were not ready to launch an immediate attack to push Germany out of Poland. The Polish military fought bravely but suffered heavy losses and fell quickly. Germany divided Poland in two, keeping half and giving half to the Soviet Union.

At the start of World War II, Germany and Britain mostly fought at sea. On April 9, 1940, Germany went north and invaded Norway and then Denmark. From there, Germany blocked northern shipping routes in the Atlantic. Norway and Denmark formed a protective barrier for Germany. In Denmark, the Germans built a huge radar network. It alerted them when British air strikes were approaching.

While Nazi Germany gobbled up countries, the Soviet Union pushed beyond Poland to grab more land, too. The Soviets invaded the Baltic States of Estonia, Latvia, and Lithuania. Then they defeated Finland. Soon, most of Europe chose sides. Across the ocean, Americans argued about which side to support. For a long time, the United States refused to get involved in the fighting.

After Nazi Germany attacked Belgium, it took over the Netherlands and crossed into France with a great deal of military force. In 1940, Germany began bombing Britain at night. Germany's air force was well-equipped and powerful. It attacked Britain's industrial cities and ports, as well as England's capital, London. German bombs fell on homes, including the royal palace.

Germany and the Soviet Union might have started the war as friends, but that didn't last. Hitler broke his promise, and Germany invaded the Soviet Union. The Germans marched until they were just twenty miles from Moscow, the capital of the Soviet Union, but t were stopped by a brutal winter. After Germany invaded, the Soviet Union joined the Allied Forces.

Nazi Germany was spread across Europe. While Germany benefited from its expansion, it also paid a price. Germany was surrounded. There were enemies on all sides. The German army was spread thin and became weaker. Germany's borders were far apart, and the territories it occupied were filled with angry people who hated Nazi rule.

The citizens of the countries occupied by Nazi Germany separated themselves into three groups. There were people who tried to ignore what was happening and simply survive the war. There were collaborators, who actively helped the enemy rule their country. Finally, there were people who fought back, taking extraordinary risks. Many were part of the **underground** army. They were called **Resistance** fighters because they pushed back against the rule of Nazi Germany. They weren't alone. People in Allied countries sent secret agents and military personnel to fight the Nazis, too.

In secret documents, sensitive information was often blacked out.

• • SPIES IN EUROPE • •

Spies were all over Europe long before World War II started. Most countries in Europe, and in other parts of the world, protected themselves by using spies to find and take secret information, called "intelligence," from other countries. They sent the intelligence to their spy agencies, which were secret parts of their militaries or governments.

Once World War II began, getting intelligence became more important than ever before. The Allied Forces wanted to know many things: How many troops did Germany have, and where? Were troops moving, and how—by train or on foot? Were the Nazis building a rocket weapon?

Britain had several spy organizations before World War II, and it quickly added more. The other side did, too. Germany's spy agency, the **Abwehr**, had been developing spies in Britain and the United States for decades. During World War II, the Germans were especially interested in knowing how far the Americans had gotten in the making of rockets and other weapons.

Once the war began, England rushed to send secret agents to live with the enemy and spy on them. This meant living in occupied territories, the places Nazi Germany had invaded and now controlled. But people who lived there spoke German, French, Danish, Dutch, and other languages. How could Britain find people who spoke foreign languages as if they were native speakers?

British spy agencies approached people whose parents had immigrated to Great Britain from other countries in Europe. The adult children of immigrants could often speak their parents' native languages. When they went back to their parents' homeland, now occupied by Nazi Germany, they could blend into the local population. Spy agencies also recruited immigrants who were fleeing the war and were willing to go back to defend their country against Nazi Germany.

Britain found people already in the occupied territories who wanted to help the Allies. Many didn't wait for Britain to recruit them but began to spy on the enemy as soon as Nazi Germany arrived. They didn't want to be ruled by Nazi Germany. They were Resistance fighters, part of underground armies, working secretly to defend their homelands. They were brave warriors and Britain used them, building a large spy network. It stretched across all of Europe and was very important in eventually winning the war.

France had a large Resistance movement filled with French people who did not want their government working with Nazi Germany. When Germany invaded, the French government quickly voted to give in and allow Germany to rule alongside a French leader. The French underground went into action. French spies worked closely with British spy agencies. Resistance fighters kept track of German troop movements, stole weapons and battle plans, and **sabotaged** German trains. They reported information to the British, and later to the Americans.

Poland had a long history of using spies. When Germany invaded Poland in 1939, the Polish government already had spy networks stretching across Europe and other parts of the world. This was the **Polish Intelligence**. Until World War II, it did not share its secret information with other countries, not even its friends. Poland also had Resistance fighters organized into the Home Army, which provided a lot of military information to help the British army. They sabotaged German supply lines, which delayed food and ammunition from getting to enemy soldiers. They killed top Nazi officials. Even more unusual, they waged long battles, fighting directly against the German army. The Warsaw Uprising was one of their most famous battles.

Over a million Resistance fighters were in the underground armies, acting as spies throughout Europe. British secret agents worked alongside Resistance movements in each country, supplying them with guns and ammunition. Brave Resistance fighters bombed convoys of German troops and sabotaged factories that made weapons. They helped bring Allied planes and people into the occupied territories. They arranged drop zones by setting up lights in dark fields at night on which Allied planes could land or British and American commandos could parachute into for special missions.

The Soviet spy organization, **NKVD** (People's Commissariat for Internal Affairs), was formed in 1917. Before World War II, the NKVD had some spies in France and England, but more spies were in Germany and Asia because the Soviet Union feared Germany or Japan would invade it.

During World War II, Europe was crowded with spies. Although German spies were everywhere, their national intelligence organization, the Abwehr, was poorly run. Many of its agents took money from the enemy and then lied about what they knew. British spy agencies used double agents. They were enemy agents who decided to switch and spy for the Allies. Double agents would send the wrong information to the German military. They often used fake intelligence reports that the British created. The reports looked real and convinced the German military that the information was true.

The **Gestapo** was the secret police of Nazi Germany. It competed with the Abwehr for money and missions. The Gestapo believed the best way to deal with a badly run German intelligence agency was to get rid of it.

•• WAR IN THE PACIFIC ••

On the other side of the globe, Japan needed natural resources, food, and a workforce. Oil, iron ore, and steel would keep its factories working. The island country made weapons to fight the war it had started with China. The United States decided to punish Japan by cutting off its supply of oil and other important materials.

After the United States stopped Japan from buying the supplies it needed, Japan launched a surprise attack against the US Navy, whose ships were docked in Pearl Harbor, Hawaii, at the US naval base. On the morning of December 7, 1941, Japan bombed Pearl Harbor, killing 2,403 American military personnel and **civilians**.

The attack on Pearl Harbor was the act of war that convinced America to get involved in the fight overseas. The United States declared war against Japan and Germany. Japan quickly sided with Germany and Italy, joining the Axis Powers. The United States joined in with the Allied Forces: Britain, France, the Soviet Union, other European nations fighting Germany, and China.

Japan had many victories at the beginning of the war. In December 1941, the Japanese bombed the US air base on Luzon, in the Philippines. Most of the planes were on the ground and were destroyed. The attack cut US air power in half. More attacks followed. By the end of December, the Japanese had wiped out most US aircraft in Asia.

The Japanese continued to win battle after battle in the Pacific until the Battle of Midway in June 1942. Midway Atoll is a submerged volcanic island with a giant reef. It is located with other atolls northwest of Hawaii, halfway between Japan and the US mainland.

During World War II, the US military used Midway Atoll as a naval air base. When the Japanese attacked, the Americans were prepared. Despite being outgunned, the US military sank all four of the Japanese Navy's attacking ships. The Battle of Midway was considered a turning point in the war.

In the southwestern Pacific Ocean, the Japanese lost to the Americans again at the Battle of Guadalcanal. The battle began in August 1942 and ended in February 1943. Finally, the Americans took the lead in the war.

US military personnel fought island by island in a long, drawn-out war. Little by little, they worked their way toward Japan.

• • SPIES IN THE PACIFIC • •

Before World War II, Japanese spies operated out of Hawaii. There were at least two spies that helped plan the attack on Pearl Harbor: Takeo Yoshikawa and Bernard Julius Otto Kuehn. You'll hear more about them in chapter 2.

During the war, the Japanese used propaganda, or false information, to try to make American soldiers lose their fighting spirit and go home. There were big battles in the war, but there were also long stretches of time between the battles when soldiers had to wait. Soldiers listened to the radio. Japan blasted radio programs out to the airwaves. These programs played American music to make the military personnel homesick, and the radio announcers were women who spoke English and told stories to upset the listeners. The soldiers called this group of female broadcasters "Tokyo Rose." You'll hear more about one of them in chapter 5.

• • US ISOLATIONISM • •

Two years after World War I ended, the League of Nations was formed to prevent another worldwide war. It was designed as a place for countries to talk over their disagreements and find solutions. The American Congress said no to joining the League of Nations, even though it was created by the then-president of the United States, Woodrow Wilson.

Congress wanted to keep the United States out of conflicts in Europe. After all, the United States had problems of its own. Later, in 1929, the stock market had crashed and by 1933 had lost most of its value. Life savings were wiped out. Businesses closed. Jobs disappeared. In the middle of America, where much of the country's food was grown, there was a drought. No rain. No crops. It was the Great Depression.

This economic depression was worldwide. The nations in Europe that had borrowed money from the United States to rebuild after World War I couldn't pay it back. Americans were angry and stopped loaning money to other countries, even to allies like England. When Europe went to war a second time, people in the United States were fed up. War had cost too much. The price of World War I had been more than money to run the military; it had been American lives.

When Germany and Japan began to push other countries around, Americans felt safe. Thousands of miles of ocean separated Europe and Asia from the United States. Back then, airplanes could not fly long distances like they can today. People traveled by ship, and the trip was long. Europe and Asia were very far away from everyday American life.

At the start of World War II, many politicians urged Americans to use their isolation from Europe to their advantage and stay out of the conflict. And they did.

• • SPIES IN THE UNITED STATES • •

There were many reasons countries spied on each other, and there still are. It was not always because nations were enemies. They might be economic competitors or even friends.

Nations that were friendly with each other sent spies to gather information. It wasn't necessarily secret information; it could be public opinion. Countries wanted to know what people in the government and on the street were really thinking, feeling, and saying to one another. Spies found out. They took what they learned and sent it to their spy agencies, who shared it with their governments.

Britain placed spies in Washington, DC, so they could influence Americans to join with the Allied Forces and fight Nazi Germany. Meanwhile, Germany had spies in the United States trying to convince Americans to support Hitler. They said a Europe unified under Nazi Germany would be good for American business.

German spies also wanted to keep track of US progress in building airplanes, rockets, and guns. When the United States entered the war in 1941, Germany needed to know exactly how powerful an enemy America would be. They gathered secret information about military bases, bridges, railroads, and factories. If there were weaknesses, the Germans wanted to plan sabotage missions. They wanted to disrupt daily life for Americans and stop the production of military supplies.

▶ ESPIONAGE BY THE NUMBERS ◀

The US ███████ coastline is 4,903 miles away from the continent of Europe. It took ███████ five or more days for a ship to cross the Atlantic.

CHAPTER 2

SPY MISSIONS

SPIES APPEARED OUT OF NOWHERE IN many cities during World War II. Where did they come from, and how did they learn to be spies?

Who recruited them for the job? What did a spy have to know?

This chapter explains how a person was chosen to become a spy, his or her training, the tools of the trade, and the impact they made on the outcome of a battle.

•• SPY QUALIFICATIONS ••

Not everyone could be a spy. Espionage demanded special talents. Working as a secret agent required skills that came from training and practice. Other abilities couldn't be taught but were part of a spy's personality. After all, a spy didn't get a day off.

Although there were no set requirements for being a spy, intelligence agencies tried to find people who could work secretly without being noticed. Spies had to blend into their surroundings. If they were mixing with high society and attending fashionable events, they had to wear the correct outfits and look comfortable in them. If they had a job in a factory, they had to wear work clothes and look and sound like everyone else there. A spy's most important skill was to blend in and not be noticed.

Spies also had to know a lot. They needed to know more than anybody else in the room, no matter what room they were in. If there was something they didn't know, they could be at a disadvantage. But having more knowledge didn't mean they would tell people all they knew. They had to have good judgment and listen more than they talked. They had to be able to get other people to talk about their work or their lives. This meant a spy had to have strong people skills, too.

What if a spy showed an emotion, made a mistake, or was caught where they didn't belong? A spy needed to be able to think quickly and be prepared. They had to be ready with explanations and excuses. What they said had to fit the situation and sound believable. Their story had to convince anyone asking them questions.

Most spies worked as drivers and secretaries, or some other common job. This meant, of course, they had to do the work of a driver or secretary. Spies working as secretaries couldn't pretend to type—they had to type, and do it well.

People who worked as spies had to be careful all the time. They lived knowing they were always at risk of being caught. If a spy had a family, their spouse and children could not know the truth. It was a double life.

•• RECRUITING SPIES ••

After World War I, many Europeans left their war-torn countries to live and work in the United States. Intelligence agencies from many different countries asked these immigrants to become spies.

It wasn't hard to find new immigrants. They tended to live, work, and be friends with other immigrants from their former countries. It was more comfortable to be with people who shared the same culture and spoke the same language. But intelligence organizations didn't openly send agents into immigrant communities to recruit spies. They didn't have recruitment offices like the military did.

One place where agents recruited was social or athletic clubs. There were many clubs in America where people from one country could come together to socialize or play a sport. There were clubs for French people, Italians, Germans, and many other nationalities. Spy agencies sent people into these clubs. They pretended they belonged there. They watched people and listened to them. They learned who had problems and what the problems were. They pretended to be friends.

Agents also recruited spies wherever important secret information was being developed, transmitted, or stored. If someone had access to information, like a secretary typing reports in an embassy or a military photographer taking pictures of maps, this person could be a target. Spies looked for people who had access to secret information, and then they looked to see if these people had weaknesses. When an agency wanted to recruit a person, they would send a spy to watch the person for weeks and become the person's friend, making the person feel safe.

After the agency knew a lot about a target, they used that information to convince the person to spy for the agency. For example, if an immigrant was unhappy with the United States, the agent would tell him it was his patriotic duty to help his home country or "motherland." If a military photographer was disappointed in his country, the agent might convince him to support the enemy and share secret documents. If a person had money problems, the agency might bribe her, offering to pay for information. If a person had a secret, the agency could threaten to expose the secret unless the person spied for them.

In the case of Germany's spy agency, the Abwehr, they also used threats. They said the agency would hurt the immigrant's family, who were still living in Germany.

After World War II began, new intelligence organizations were formed. There was a great rush to bring on as many secret agents as possible. Spies were needed behind enemy lines, in neutral territories, and in their own countries.

One of the new spy organizations was in the United States. Before the war, the United States didn't have a government spy agency like many other countries did. It only used spies if there was a special mission. During the war, the United States created the **OSS**, Office of Strategic Services, to plan spy missions in enemy territory.

The OSS looked for people who spoke one or more foreign languages well. If the agency needed a spy to go into Nazi-occupied France, the agency wanted a person who spoke French as if he or she had grown up there. A spy couldn't sound like an American who had learned French. An American accent would give a spy away and put them in danger. It helped if the person was familiar with the culture. In this case, it meant knowing how French people in Paris or in the countryside would speak, act, and dress.

The OSS and Britain's Special Operations Executive (**SOE**) would approach people who were fleeing occupied countries and ask them to go back into danger. Many men and women left the safety of their new homes and returned to their countries to help the Allies defeat Nazi Germany. They went for different reasons: They were patriotic, they wanted revenge against the Nazis, and a few wanted the challenge or adventure. They performed many espionage activities, including bringing messages back and forth between members of the Allied Forces and Resistance fighters.

The British also recruited at college campuses, looking for patriotic people who spoke other languages. They needed to be willing to cross into enemy territory and pretend to be a different nationality. Or they might work at an embassy, stealing information and reporting it to the Allies.

There were many different types of spies, and governments needed all sorts of people to fill those jobs. When an espionage mission required a special skill, the intelligence agencies worked to find the right person. Sometimes this led British intelligence organizations to go to prisons to recruit their spies. The best professional lock pickers and safecrackers were there.

Not all spies went into enemy territory. Some worked in offices and universities in the United States and Great Britain. The British and the Americans needed special minds to work secretly on breaking **codes** the enemy used to hide messages, and on developing codes for the Allies to use. Allied intelligence services searched universities to find brilliant students and professors to do code work. The United States also worked with Native Americans, who were some of the best **code talkers** in the world.

Sometimes agencies recruited professionals who traveled often, like an international banker, a journalist, or a film star. These people might hear and see things that the agencies wanted to know. Or they might be asked to meet with the agencies' contacts to deliver or pick up a package.

All spy agencies, from Britain's MI6 to Germany's Abwehr, looked for people who understood what was going on in the world and realized the importance of the job. They had to have an interest in international affairs or strong feelings of patriotism.

•• SPY JOBS ••

Spies were placed anywhere and everywhere, sometimes in the most unlikely places.

Spies often worked for powerful people. They had to be where important, secret information was. When spies found information that could be useful to their intelligence agencies, they recorded it or memorized it, then passed it on to another agent. They did all this without being noticed.

Many times, spies spread propaganda, information that was one-sided or untrue. They did it to make people question the war effort. They created unrest and distrust. They spread rumors, which made people unhappy and ruined the morale of soldiers. They worked at radio stations and newspapers, where information was received and transmitted all day. They used the news to their advantage.

A spy might have been a fisherman who watched ships going in and out of ports. They might have been a file clerk who had access to building plans. Spies worked at plants making airplane parts, and their reports helped their spy agencies keep track of the size of an air force. Spies worked at food companies and shoe factories, letting their spy agencies know if the military ordered large quantities of food or boots and where they were being sent. Anything that might reveal information about weapons and troops, how big they were and where they were going, could be useful to the enemy.

Spies had common jobs like being a waiter in a restaurant or a shoe polisher in an office building. They overheard conversations and reported them to their spy agencies. Some spies drove officers in the army. They reported the number of troops and where they were located. Cleaning people in government offices could take scraps of paper thrown into trash baskets and give them to their superiors.

Valuable intelligence could be found anywhere, from a post office, to a school, to a city planning office. Spies went everywhere there was information. Even casual conversations between friends or acquaintances could reveal important data.

Sometimes spies didn't just collect information. They also gave out fake intelligence. They could give out reports of false numbers of soldiers or plans of attacks that would never happen. They caused confusion with the enemy, giving them information that made them send troops to the wrong place.

Some very smart spies worked on breaking enemy codes. They worked with the enemy's special **cipher** or secret coding machines. They converted, or translated, the secret messages into the original form so they could understand what the secret was. Sometimes it was the location and date of an upcoming attack.

A spy could be anyone, anywhere.

•• SPY SCHOOLS ••

Intelligence agencies needed more spies during World War II, which also meant they needed to train people in the skills of espionage. They built new spy schools. The first secret training school in North America was **Special Training School 103**. It was quickly nicknamed Camp X. It was in Canada, thirty miles from the American border.

Britain and Canada built the school in a remote place in Canada on the shores of Lake Ontario. It seemed the perfect place to create a hideaway to teach people how to become spies. When the school opened in 1941, the United States hadn't joined the war yet, so the school could not be on American soil. However, it was close enough to the United States to give Americans easy access to the teaching facilities.

Over five hundred agents from all the Allied nations went to school at Camp X throughout the war. Some were recruited straight from colleges, others from the armed forces. They came from all walks of life and from different parts of society.

They learned useful skills, such as **unarmed combat**, sabotage, and how to find new people to recruit as spies to widen their networks. They used real explosives and had to crawl under barbed wire while real bullets were being shot at them.

They were taught about explosives, coding, weapons, and the use of disguises. However, the most important lesson was that the enemy is ruthless, and they had to be, too. Their training was ten weeks long.

Germany had a spy school on an estate near Berlin, Germany. The students there were taught to make and use explosives. They were given spy identities and learned their new backgrounds. They were not allowed to speak German, only English. They read American newspapers and magazines so they knew all about American culture. Their training was done in three weeks.

By 1942, the United States was training spies on American soil. They were learning survival techniques to use behind enemy lines.

The most important part of Camp X was a place called Hydra. It was named after the many-headed serpent from Greek mythology. Camp X ████████ Hydra was a communication center where recruits trained in code breaking. Hydra played an important role, receiving transmissions ████████████ twenty-four hours a day, seven days a week. Messages from ████████ everywhere were sent there for decoding.

• • SPIES AND BIG BATTLES • •

Spies were often used in planning and fighting major battles.

Many Japanese and American spies were hidden on islands in the Pacific. Without being seen, they used binoculars to keep track of enemy ships and aircraft. Then they reported the movements of enemy troops to their agencies and the military. The information helped the military decide where and how to launch important battles.

During the planning stage of a battle, spies could be used to send false information to the enemy. Instead of transmitting or delivering a message that had the correct information about what was planned, they would make up fake information to send. In this case, a message might say there was a plan to attack the enemy's troops at a location that was not the real location. To prepare for the attack, the enemy would move its troops to the wrong location and away from the area where the attack was actually going to take place. The Allied Forces did this before the Invasion of Normandy, code named **D-Day**. It was one of the most significant battles of the war.

Spies were also important on the battlefield. They could make the difference between victory and defeat. Native American code talkers were recruited and used on the battlefield. Their languages, such as Cree, Apache, Comanche, and others, were not taught in schools. Many of the words could not be translated. Native American languages were so different and unknown that they made perfect secret codes.

When military orders were sent out using a Native American language, the commanding officer sending it relied on a Native American code talker to code the message, and the commanding officer receiving it used a Native American code talker to translate the message from code into English.

While Nazi **code breakers** could **decipher**, or figure out, regular codes, they were unable to understand messages sent in Native American languages. The US military communicated battle plans in near total secrecy because messages sent in Native American languages were virtually unbreakable.

•• D-DAY ••

The Allied Invasion of Normandy, also known as D-Day, is a perfect example of how spies were used to give the enemy fake information about an attack. Nazi Germany knew the Allied Forces were getting ready to invade German-occupied Europe. The Germans wanted information about Allied troops, such as how many soldiers there were and where they were.

Britain "turned" many spies working for Germany into double agents working for the Allies. One pair, Mutt and Jeff, secretly switched sides. They reported to their German **handler** that the Allies were preparing to invade far north toward Scandinavia. The Allies created fake weather reports that claimed the cold northern weather was affecting their tanks. The Germans believed this fake information. They moved troops and tanks to the north and weakened their troops in Normandy, the true location of the invasion.

There were also fake reports that said the Allies were gathering troops and tanks in southern England for an invasion of southern France. To convince the Germans these reports were true, the Allies placed tanks and troops in cities in southern England. But the tanks and troops were decoys, or fake objects, such as inflatable tanks, canvas army vehicles, and dummy soldiers. These false reports and well-placed decoys deceived the Germans. They sent tanks and troops to southern France, away from Normandy.

When the Allies attacked Nazi Germany, they invaded German-occupied France at Normandy. They faced fewer German troops there because some had been sent away to the false locations. Still, the battle was not quick. The Allies needed the help of another spy, this one a Spanish spy pretending to work for Germany. He told Hitler that the Allied attack on Normandy wasn't the big invasion. He said there was a larger invasion planned in the north. His false reports caused the Germans to delay bringing their troops from the north down to Normandy, and the Allied Forces won this extremely important battle.

•• PEARL HARBOR ••

Hawaii is halfway between the US mainland and Japan. Before Hawaii became a state, it had close ties to the United States, which built a naval base at Pearl Harbor in Hawaii. It housed a fleet of ships along with all the sailors assigned to them and the military personnel working to maintain the base. On December 7, 1941, hundreds of Japanese planes—dive bombers, high bombers, torpedo bombers, and fighter bombers— attacked Pearl Harbor. All the American ships were damaged and half of them sunk.

Before Japan attacked Pearl Harbor, they put Japanese spies in Hawaii. The exact number is unknown, but two have been identified. Takeo Yoshikawa was a Japanese naval officer working undercover, meaning "in secret," at a Japanese diplomatic office in Hawaii. Diplomats handle relations between governments. While not all diplomats are spies, some spies are in or near diplomatic offices.

Takeo Yoshikawa watched Pearl Harbor. He took notes on the US Navy ships that moved in and out of the ports. He did this without hiding. Then he sent his reports to his spy agency.

Another spy helped Japan prepare for the attack against Pearl Harbor. It was Bernard Julius Otto Kuehn, a wealthy German agent living in Hawaii. After Kuehn secretly reported to his spy agency that the entire fleet of US ships was docked in Pearl Harbor, the Japanese military launched the surprise attack.

► **ESPIONAGE BY THE NUMBERS** ◄

Bernard Julius Otto Kuehn used a total of ▮▮▮▮ eight codes. He communicated by hanging clothing and bedsheets ▮▮▮▮ on his laundry line. When he hung certain clothes on his line at a certain time of day, it meant the battleships were ▮▮ all in the harbor.

CHAPTER 3

SPY GEAR

SPIES WERE RECRUITED FOR MANY reasons, but one of the most important reasons was their ability to think on their feet and make things up as they went along. With very little training, they entered the dangerous world of espionage and put their lives at risk. They depended on their own skills to keep them safe. But in addition to their skills, spies also relied on special equipment. They used creative, sometimes crudely made devices to help them do their job and protect themselves from the enemy. These tools had to blend in and not draw attention. This chapter will explore some of the special gear a spy needed to survive.

•• WEAPONS ••

One of the most popular weapons used by spies was a **coal grenade**, a small bomb that looked like a lump of coal. The coal grenade was first used in the Civil War in the United States. It was made by hollowing out a piece of iron, and then shaping it and painting it to look like an ordinary piece of coal. Last, it was filled with explosives and used as a bomb.

In the early to mid-1900s, many buildings, trains, and homes were heated by coal fires. Spies would drop these explosive devices near a building that was fueled by coal. Once thrown into a furnace, they would explode, destroying an entire factory or office building.

Both British and American spies employed this weapon during the war. An agent could simply carry the coal grenade in his hand and drop it in a pile of coal waiting to be shoveled into a building.

Agents of Nazi Germany had coal grenades when they invaded the United States in 1942. It was a secret mission, Operation Pastorius. German U-boats, or submarines, carried Nazi agents to beaches on Long

Island in New York and on Florida's coast. They landed and planned to sabotage American targets: factories, railroads, the water system, and coal-fired industrial buildings. But before they could use their coal grenades and other explosives, one of the spies turned himself in and stopped the attack.

Another way spies hid bombs was to stuff dead rats with explosives and then place them near factories or enemy bases. Soldiers or workers would come across the dead rodents and throw them into a fire to destroy them, setting off the explosives. Eventually, the workers were afraid that any rat might be booby trapped, and the rats were left to rot. The decaying corpses served as another weapon of sorts, as the dead rodents spread disease.

Other weapons could be stashed in jacket lapels, sleeves, pencils, pens, and other places people wouldn't think to search. During World War II, many people smoked cigarettes or pipes. A special smoking pipe was invented that was really a pistol. There were exploding cigarette cases. Writing pens were also designed with hidden guns inside. These tools meant spies could

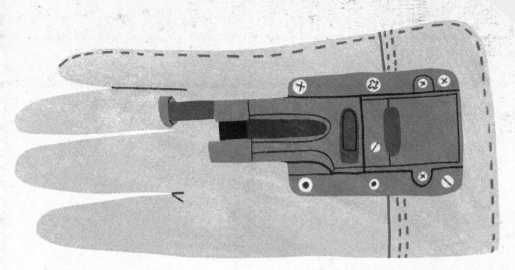

A GLOVE PISTOL

always be armed. Agents could now protect themselves when in an enemy office or at a social event.

An American gun factory manufactured a single-shot pistol attached to the inside of a thick glove for the Allied Forces. When a person wearing this glove was involved in a fistfight, the gun would go off when they punched the other person. While it was good for only one shot, at that close range it rarely missed and the results were deadly.

Spies found creative ways to communicate. They had to leave written messages in secret places that would only be found by the spy who was their contact. There were many hiding places.

Spies removed spikes from the top of fences, hollowed them out, and put them back so no one noticed. When they had a message, they hid it inside one of the spikes.

They also pushed written messages behind loose bricks in the wall of specially chosen buildings. Agents would leave a coded message squeezed behind a loose brick to be retrieved later by another spy who knew exactly where to look.

Spies also used clotheslines in a creative way. They hung clothes on the line in a specific order to create a coded message. Another agent would read it and pass it along to the spy agency.

Agents communicated by moving flowerpots on their porches into special spots, so only another trained spy could understand that a message was being delivered.

Spies also needed tools to transmit, or send, information secretly. **Morse code** uses dots (short sounds) and dashes (longer sounds) to transmit a message. Spies used radio receivers, wireless sets, and **transmitters** to send secret messages. Being caught with a radio transmitter behind enemy lines meant certain execution. Spies hid the different pieces of radio equipment in everything from cigar boxes to cookie tins. This allowed an agent to keep a two-way radio on a kitchen counter in their home, stashed in a specially made box of cookies.

A RADIO TRANSMITTER

When there was limited electricity due to blackouts or destroyed power stations, spies could use bicycles to keep transmitters running. By connecting a generator to a stationary bike, a spy could ride it to generate the electricity needed to transmit their message.

Walter Zapp, a German inventor, created a miniature camera in the early 1930s. The camera was no bigger than four inches, so small it fit in the palm of a hand. It could be stored in a matchbox. Spies working as secretaries or assistants could photograph important information and then hide both the camera and the

MINIATURE CAMERA EQUIPMENT

negatives hard-to-find places, like inside a pen, a shoe heel, or even a pair of fake teeth. Some agents even had specially fitted false teeththat allowed them to travel with stolen information hidden inside.

Spies had shoes with hidden compartments for knives, messages, microfilm, and paper money. Agents had to have a lot of cash to pay off informants. Money was used to buy information.

Another useful tool was invisible ink. Both the Allied Forces and the Nazis were working on finding more ways to make ink undetectable. Special chemicals, blood, and urine were used to hide messages from being read. Exposing a suspected letter to heat, ultraviolet light, or iodine vapors could reveal the message, so each government was hard at work finding better ways to write invisible messages and escape detection.

•• SABOTAGE ••

Sabotage is a deliberate act to destroy, ruin, or interrupt normal life and create chaos. Spies used a number of devices for sabotage.

Limpet mines were special magnetic bombs that could be attached to the metal side of an enemy ship or bridge. Named for the little limpet sea creatures that attach themselves to coral in the ocean, these explosive

LIMPET MINES ATTACHED TO THE SIDE OF A SHIP

devices could be stuck on a ship docked in a harbor.
When it exploded, the ship sank. The British needed
a way to attach these little bombs to ships and bridges.
They had to devise a system for a person to swim
underwater undetected.

The Allies purchased a new device that allowed agents
to breathe underwater for missions of destruction. It was
like scuba gear, but it was less bulky. Most important,
there were no air bubbles for the enemy to see. It was

invented by a doctor, who later joined the OSS. The inventor demonstrated it in a swimming pool for the British SOE and American OSS. This underwater breathing invention enabled secret agents to attach the new limpet mines to enemy vessels without being seen.

Allied intelligence organizations researched ways for spies to conduct sabotage on land without leaving footprints that could lead the Nazis to find them. They invented special shoes that looked like the soles of bare feet. Each pair of rubber molds could be strapped over

THIS DEVICE ALLOWED
AGENTS TO BREATHE
UNDERWATER

OVERSHOES THAT LOOKED LIKE BARE FEET

the agent's shoes. They would disguise a spy's footprints and make it harder for Germans to find them after they sabotaged supply lines or anything else. Instead of footprints that looked like the boots of a soldier, these shoes would make footprints of someone wearing no shoes. It would look like a barefoot peasant had been running around. The Resistance movement used this shoe invention to disguise their work and send the Germans after the wrong person.

In a spy's world, nothing was as it seemed. A pen was not a pen, but a gun. Shoes were not for walking, but for hiding messages. Jewelry was more valuable for what was stashed underneath the gems. The same was true of music, musicians, and instruments. Orchestra music was very popular during the war. Musicians traveled through German-occupied territories, carrying instrument cases on their way to entertain the officers of Nazi Germany, but when a spy carried a violin case, it held tools of sabotage, like wire cutters, explosives, and funny shoes to disguise footprints.

German spies were known to create bombs that looked like tins of candy, chocolates, shaving brushes, and stuffed animals. They could be used as emergency hand grenades, but their main purpose was to **assassinate** people. These deadly treats would be delivered to unsuspecting victims in their own homes or offices. The Nazis developed a special candy bar for

THIS PIPE IS ALSO A PISTOL

just this purpose. They coated steel with a thin layer of chocolate and set the detonator of the hidden bomb to go off when the person broke the chocolate bar. It was intended to be smuggled into the house of the British royal family, but it was discovered long before it could be used.

•• MAPS ••

Soldiers who were captured by the enemy and held in **prisoner-of-war camps** were allowed to receive mail from their families.

Sometimes their mail was ordinary. Other times, letters, playing cards, board games, and music sent to them had been secretly altered to help the soldiers escape.

MAPS ARE HIDDEN IN THESE PLAYING CARDS

Inside board games, like Monopoly, a soldier might find compasses, maps, and German money. Playing cards could have messages and maps glued under the faces of the jacks, queens, and kings.

Families liked to send records so soldiers could listen to music. But records were made of plastic and were fragile, so they often broke. A broken record was sometimes filled with money, maps, and documents like fake identity papers.

•• TOOLS TO ESCAPE DETECTION ••

During World War II, everyone was required to have identity papers on them at all times. Spies needed to carry documents proving who they said they were. They carried multiple sets of passports and other documents to change their identity as needed. Every government intelligence organization had many people, often gifted artists, creating fake passports and identity papers, as well as counterfeit money. These papers had to fool anyone who examined them, and they often did.

Sometimes a spy was caught. Agencies invented ways to avoid being questioned by the enemy. If an agent decided to die rather than risk revealing information when tortured, there was poison.

Poison was often hidden in everyday items like buttons, rings, and

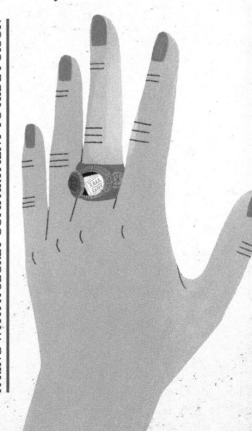

A RING WITH A SECRET COMPARTMENT TO HIDE POISON

necklaces. When captured, an agent could pop a stone from their ring or necklace into their mouth. If they were dead, they avoided the pain of torture and the real possibility of revealing other agents.

Of course, if an agent had an opportunity to take a cigarette break before being captured, he might offer the enemy agent a cigarette. There was an exploding cigarette case that would

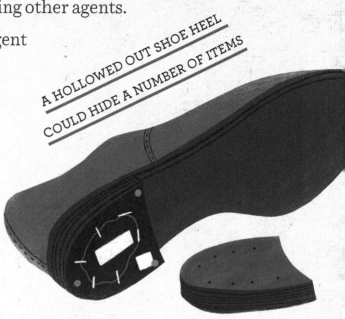

A HOLLOWED OUT SHOE HEEL COULD HIDE A NUMBER OF ITEMS

have been very useful at this moment. There were also cigarettes laced with a drug that caused the smoker to relax and tell all secrets. Escaping wasn't guaranteed, but good spy tools made it more possible.

•• CLOTHING ••

A spy's choice of clothing could mean the difference between life and death. Seamstresses were recruited and sworn to secrecy. They created entire wardrobes for agents. A simple oversight, such as a zipper with a British or American logo, might be noticed and make people suspicious.

Only the very wealthy had new suits in Germany during the war. If an agent was going into Germany and pretending to be an ordinary person, he or she needed clothing that appeared ordinary. No part of an outfit could look new. Technicians from England knew how to make clothing look worn and smell used. They rubbed sandpaper on the material to fray it and sewed on old buttons. They darkened seams with petroleum jelly.

At that time, seams on garments were sewn differently in France and Germany. The British wanted to make sure an agent would blend in and look like they belonged. Everything from collar style to the thickness of the thread used was changed to match what was popular in Germany and France. Even buttonholes were redone to match the styles there. Each outfit had to be unique, and a lot of work was done to prevent the agents from looking like they had all gotten their clothing at the same store.

Female spies were told not to color their hair or wear makeup or nail polish. In war-torn Europe, people didn't have time or money for those things. In the occupied territories, civilians didn't have fancy haircuts. Agents got haircuts before they left on missions, so their hairstyles matched the locals.

Dentists in London replaced British fillings with gold teeth to match the way teeth were repaired in France and in other occupied territories. If an agent was caught by the Germans and questioned, every part of his or her identity had to match the country they claimed to live in.

Shoes, pajamas, mustaches, luggage—every detail had to be considered to keep an agent safe. The smallest error could reveal an agent's true identity and result in torture and death.

▶ ESPIONAGE BY THE NUMBERS ◀

At the height of the war, the ██████ British provided entire ██████ wardrobes for sixteen agents each day. By 1944, more than 90,000 ██████████ articles of clothing were provided.

CHAPTER 4

<u>SECRET ARMIES</u>

AS THE WORLD ERUPTED INTO A WAR, each government realized it had to find new ways to fight the enemy. Information became a key element in victory, so one by one, each nation developed spy agencies to handle this information. They needed them for a variety of espionage activities: intelligence gathering, sabotage, communicating with Resistance fighters, giving out false information to the enemy, creating unrest in enemy-occupied territories, and managing the famous Double Cross System. The following is a list of organizations that recruited and developed the spy programs.

•• BRITAIN: SPECIAL OPERATIONS EXECUTIVE (SOE), MILITARY INTELLIGENCE SECTION 5 (MI5), MILITARY INTELLIGENCE SECTION 6 (MI6) ••

Britain formed the **SOE** in July 1940 to use spies to fight the Nazis. Secret agents were planted in German-occupied Europe to report information to the SOE. They also brought weapons to local Resistance fighters, coordinated sabotage of German supply lines and German operations, or went on missions alone.

The SOE employed agents from all social backgrounds and walks of life. They were famous for employing women for spy missions, which was an unpopular idea at the time. They also recruited criminals from jails to help with espionage. The SOE operated in all the territories occupied by the Axis Powers.

MI5 was created by the British in the early 1900s. It was a domestic organization, which means it operated in the country. It was split into an army section and a naval division. The naval division worked on spying to discover the strength of the German Navy before World War I.

The army division originally worked with the local British Metropolitan Police Service to identify all foreign spies working inside England. A special branch was created to handle arrests, investigations, and questioning.

MI6 is also known as the Secret Intelligence Service (SIS). The organization was created in 1909 and is still active today. It is the foreign arm of the intelligence service of the government, which means it works outside the country. MI6 gathers information and reports it to the foreign secretary. It is known for actively feeding false information to the Germans.

MI6 also worked in **cryptology**, breaking the codes that enemies used to hide their communications. MI6 intercepted Nazi communications, translated secret messages, and worked at code breaking, in general. The Royal Air Force (RAF) Photographic Reconnaissance Unit was responsible for taking photographs of the enemy from the air.

•• THE DOUBLE CROSS ••

MI5 was famous for turning spies into double agents. When MI5 discovered an enemy spy, it gave them a choice: Go to jail or start working for the Allies. This program was called the **Double Cross** System. British intelligence found many German spies and turned them into double agents. The double agents then gave their German spy agencies reports with false information to mislead them.

It was a highly successful plan and played an important role in the Allied Invasion of Normandy, code named D-Day.

•• THE UNITED STATES: OFFICE OF STRATEGIC SERVICES (OSS) ••

The United States formed the **OSS** during World War II to send agents behind enemy lines to spy for all the branches of the American military.

The OSS had stations all over the world, with agents providing information on Germany's air force, troops, submarines, and programs for chemical and biological warfare. The Switzerland station worked with Resistance fighters in both Italy and France.

The OSS recruited smart people who could operate independently and think fast. Many celebrities, actors, authors, and athletes were members of the organization.

▶ ▶ ▶ DID YOU KNOW? ◀ ◀ ◀

Even though ████ MI5 was vital to the war effort, World War II was one of the lowest points in its history. The staff was reduced to only ████ thirty-six agents. Aerial bombings destroyed most of the agency's files, and it had to leave its ███████ headquarters.

•• GERMANY: THE ABWEHR, REICH MAIN SECURITY OFFICE (RSHA) ••

The Abwehr was the German intelligence agency formed in 1920. At the end of World War I, Germany surrendered and signed the Treaty of Versailles, which said that Germany was not allowed to form a spy organization. Germany created the Abwehr anyway, claiming it was a necessary defense against foreign spies.

The German Abwehr grew in power. It employed spies and set up offices all over the world to gather information. Its spies were everywhere, from Mexico to London. By 1942, German agents were operating inside America's largest gun manufacturers.

The German Abwehr captured many foreign agents and forced them to give false information to their spy agencies. It is believed, however, that British intelligence organizations knew their agents were being used, so the British fed fake information back to the Germans.

When the Nazis rose to power in Germany, they developed a secret police force, the Gestapo. A branch of the Gestapo was the **RSHA**. It was an intelligence organization for the Gestapo that conducted investigations and spied on foreigners within Germany and on German citizens. It helped spread Nazi beliefs and kept track of public opinion. The RSHA was also responsible for many deaths.

The Abwehr and the RSHA competed for power. The RSHA thought the Abwehr was poorly organized and corrupt. It would not use information gathered by the Abwehr, even when it thought that information was correct.

Many German Abwehr officials were unhappy with the Nazi party, and some tried to assassinate Hitler. They were unsuccessful. Hitler ended the Abwehr in 1944 and the RSHA took over its role.

•• FRENCH RESISTANCE ••

In 1940, Germany invaded France. The French government collaborated with the Germans, and many French people were angry at this betrayal. Small groups of fighters formed. They published newspapers, fought, and sabotaged Nazi Germany's transportation, communication, and electrical power. They were a great source of information for the Allied Forces.

The French Resistance movement had people from many different backgrounds. They created escape networks, helping people get out of German-occupied territories.

Resistance fighters lived in constant danger. Sometimes French people turned in Resistance fighters to the Nazis, and the fighters were arrested, tortured, and executed. Germans set up curfews, a time in the evening when non-Germans were required to stay off the streets. If the German military or police discovered a person outside after curfew for any reason, the person could be arrested, no questions asked. This was true for anyone loitering—meaning waiting around in public, at any time of day. Resistance fighters had to live as simply and quietly as possible.

• • RUSSIA: PEOPLE'S COMMISSARIAT FOR INTERNAL AFFAIRS (NKVD) • •

The NKVD was created in 1917 as a police organization overseeing criminals, prisons, and labor camps. The NKVD did both criminal police work and secret police work. In their role as a secret police organization, the

Soviet NKVD was responsible for the deaths of many innocent civilians.

Originally allied with Germany, the Soviet NKVD met with Nazi Germany's Gestapo to plan the invasion of Poland in 1939. After the Germans invaded the Soviet Union, however, the Soviet NKVD had a new responsibility. It went to the front lines of the war against Germany and stopped Soviet soldiers from deserting, or leaving the military without permission. The Soviet NKVD also carried out sabotage missions in enemy territory.

• • POLISH INTELLIGENCE • •

Polish Intelligence was a well-established, expert intelligence organization long before World War I. It generally did not share intelligence information with foreign countries. However, when Nazi Germany and the Soviet Union invaded Poland in 1939, Polish Intelligence rushed to Britain and France. It shared long-held secrets. It played a major role in cracking

German code machines, which let the British know what the Germans were planning.

During World War II, Polish Intelligence included 400,000 Resistance fighters in Poland. They provided a great deal of valuable information to the Allies about the German invasion of the Soviet Union. They had information about the movement of submarines in and out of ports in German-occupied France. They told the Allies about Nazi Germany's secret rocket program. They also told them about **concentration camps**, where millions of Jews from Poland and other countries were killed.

The true contribution of Polish Intelligence wasn't acknowledged until 2005.

▶ ESPIONAGE BY THE NUMBERS ◀

The British Special ▮▮▮▮ Operations Executive (SOE) employed or controlled more than ▮▮ 13,000 people. At least 3,200 ▮▮▮▮ were women.

CHAPTER 5

SUPER SPIES

AFTER SO MANY COUNTRIES CREATED intelligence organizations, they raced to fill them with secret agents to do the work. Many people were recruited, from the wealthy to criminals. Anyone who had a needed skill was whisked away to secret training camps to learn the art of espionage. Some of the names on this list will be familiar and some may surprise you. Athletes, journalists, authors, and lawyers, both male and female, joined the ranks of the secret army, very often hiding the truth from the people closest to them.

•• VIRGINIA HALL ••

Virginia Hall was an American woman who spied for both the British and the Americans against the Germans. Virginia Hall worked for Britain's SOE in the early years of the war.

Hall lived in Paris when the war broke out. She immediately became involved, driving an ambulance to bring in wounded French soldiers. She left France and traveled to England after Nazi Germany occupied France.

In August 1941, Virginia Hall volunteered to join Britain's SOE. She learned spy craft: weaponry, unarmed combat, secret communications, and

VIRGINIA HALL

the art of not getting caught and staying alive while doing dangerous activities. While she worked as a journalist, she was also fighting the Germans. Some of her code names were Marie Monin, Germaine, Diane, Marie of Lyon, Camille, and Nicolas.

The Germans knew there was a female spy but couldn't identify her. They called her "Artemis." Artemis was the Greek goddess of hunting. The Germans also referred to her as the "limping lady," because of her artificial leg. Virginia Hall's leg had been amputated when she was younger after a hunting accident in Turkey. It gave her a lot of trouble walking at times. Hall gave her wooden leg the name "Cuthbert."

In March 1944, Hall joined the United States' OSS, which sent her to France with a cover, or fake identity. Her assignment was to be a **liaison**, a link between the French Resistance and the Allied Forces. She secretly carried messages and other communications from one to the other.

Virginia Hall set up spy networks. She recruited French people to hide Allied military personnel who had parachuted in or escaped from prisoner-of-war camps by taking them into their homes. She arranged drop zones where weapons were supplied to the Resistance fighters. She trained the spies in her network to make surprise attacks and then escape.

Virginia Hall was brave, smart, and inventive. She continued to supply information to the Allied Forces until the end of the war. After the war, she spent fifteen years working for America's Central Intelligence Agency (CIA), which was formed to take the place of the OSS. She was the only civilian woman awarded the Distinguished Service Cross medal in World War II.

• • RICHARD SORGE, AKA RAMSAY • •

Richard Sorge was born to a German father and Russian mother. The family moved to Germany in the early 1900s. Richard Sorge enlisted in the German army during World War I. He grew disappointed with German politics, decided he liked **communism** more, and moved to the communist Soviet Union.

As early as 1920, Richard Sorge was recruited by the Soviets to spy on Germany. He moved to Frankfurt, Germany, to gather intelligence under the cover of being a journalist. He wrote for a German newspaper.

His code name was Ramsay, and he was considered one of the best spies in the world.

In 1929, he was ordered by his Soviet intelligence superiors to join the Nazi party and stop associating with communists. They wanted the Nazis to accept and trust him. After he joined the Nazi party, his Soviet superiors directed him to get an assignment in Japan. He needed to arrange for his German newspaper to send him to Japan to report the news from there. The Soviets wanted him to set up an

RICHARD SORGE

intelligence network by recruiting informants and placing spies in jobs near, or with, important leaders in Japan.

In 1931, Japan invaded Manchuria, a section of China. The Soviet Union believed this aggressive action threatened its own eastern border. Richard Sorge went back and forth from Berlin to Tokyo, establishing himself as a trusted senior newspaper reporter. He convinced German readers that he was anti-communist. Meanwhile, his network of spies and informants stole documents from the prime minister of Japan and gave them to the Soviets.

The Germans believed Richard Sorge was a true Nazi. He was so convincing, the Germans grew to depend on his opinion of Japanese politics and culture. He was fluent in Japanese. They believed he understood the way Japanese people thought, especially those in government positions. The Germans came to trust him so much, they gave him free access to all their information, including secrets.

While living in Japan, Richard Sorge reported to the Soviet intelligence agency that the Germans were more of a threat to the Soviet Union than the Japanese. He wanted to move back to Germany and be a secret agent there.

Both the Germans and Japanese began to suspect him. In 1941, the Nazis started to monitor his communications. The Germans decided he was loyal, but the Japanese continued to watch his activities. Richard Sorge was caught by the Japanese secret police and hanged in November 1944.

• • FRITZ KOLBE, AKA GEORGE WOOD • •

Fritz Kolbe was a German diplomat who became a spy for the Americans during World War II. Fritz Kolbe was born to working-class parents with strong, "always-do-the-right-thing" values. He joined a youth movement in Germany that was anti-Nazi.

Fritz Kolbe became a clerk for the German foreign office in Madrid, Spain, and then in Warsaw, Poland. In 1937, he was assigned to Cape Town, South Africa, where he met other Germans who were anti-Nazi. He refused to join the Nazi party, so he wasn't promoted to better jobs, but his superiors trusted him because he worked hard.

Fritz Kolbe became a clerical assistant. The person he worked for was a liaison to the military. As a liaison, this person was a link between the German government and the German military. Fritz Kolbe's job was to read each

FRITZ KOLBE

message that came into the office and pass the most important ones to his superior. Many of these messages were secret communications.

Fritz Kolbe's opinion of the Nazis had not changed. He was against them and their plans. By 1941, Fritz Kolbe decided to help the Allies. He wanted the war to end, and he wanted concentration camps to be shut down. He stole blank passports so Jews could use them to escape the Nazis. He passed secret information to the

French Resistance. When he discovered a German spy was working in the Swedish embassy, he told the British. The spy was arrested.

In 1943, Fritz Kolbe became a diplomatic **courier**. Now he could carry secret papers without being caught. He brought copies to the British, but they didn't trust him. Kolbe went to the Americans and offered to work with them. His code name was George Wood, and he gave them thousands of documents. He never took any payment for his work. Fritz Kolbe was considered one of the best secret agents ever.

• • JOHN MOE AND TOR GLAD, AKA MUTT AND JEFF • •

John Moe and Tor Glad were lifelong friends. John Moe was born in London, but his family moved to Norway when he was a boy. Tor Glad was born in Oslo, Norway. Norway declared itself neutral at the start of World War II, but Nazi Germany invaded. The German spy agency, the Abwehr, hired the friends to spy for Germany, and sent them to Scotland.

In 1941, the two traveled by seaplane and life raft to Scotland. Their assignment was to transmit information to the German Abwehr and sabotage factories and other important places in Great Britain. To do this, they needed to find a place to live in Scotland and settle into the community. Instead, they immediately went to the local police and said they were German spies.

JOHN MOE AND TOR GLAD

Britain's MI5 questioned them, and then convinced them to work for the British. John Moe and Tor Glad were given the code names Mutt and Jeff. Over the next three years, the British fed them false information about the plans for the Invasion of Normandy, or D-Day. Moe and Glad then gave this false information to the Nazis. Their work helped the Allied Forces defeat Nazi Germany.

•• MARIA KRYSTYNA JANINA STARBEK, AKA CHRISTINE GRANVILLE ••

Maria Krystyna Janina Starbek was born in Poland. Her mother was a wealthy Jewish woman and her father was a Polish nobleman. Starbek had an upper-class childhood and went to college. She was in England, traveling abroad with her husband, when Nazi Germany invaded Poland.

In 1940, Maria Starbek convinced Britain's SOE to allow her to ski into Poland. She wanted to tell the Resistance fighters that the British were coming to help, to encourage them to keep fighting. The SOE gave her the code name Christine Granville, and over the years she went on many assignments.

MARIA KRYSTYNA JANINA STARBEK

Maria Starbek helped put together a network of spies that extended beyond Poland. The spies mostly carried messages and Starbek smuggled out reports to the British regularly. She also sabotaged the main communications on the Danube River and provided important information on oil transports headed to Germany.

In 1944, the British SOE sent Maria Starbek to France, under the code name Madame Pauline. She joined the French Resistance. In the mountains, she met with Polish soldiers, who were fighting for the Germans. She convinced the Polish soldiers to desert, or leave the army. Then she met with the German soldiers who had been fighting alongside the Polish soldiers. She convinced them to surrender to the Allies.

Maria Starbek was jailed several times, but she managed to escape or be released. Once she bit her tongue until it bled to fool the guards into thinking she had a contagious disease. Another time, when she and her friends were caught, she claimed her uncle was a British general and bargained her way out. She helped her friends pull off a daring escape.

Maria Starbek was charming, intelligent, and brave. Winston Churchill, the prime minister of Great Britain, said she was his favorite female spy.

•• IVA TOGURI, AKA TOKYO ROSE ••

Iva Toguri grew up in the United States, the child of immigrants who moved from Japan. After college, when she was in her early twenties, she agreed to go to Japan to help her sick aunt. According to Toguri, she didn't speak Japanese, and didn't like the food or anything else in Japan. When her parents told her to return to the United States, Iva Toguri was happy to leave. But relations between the United States and Japan were failing fast. Toguri was having problems getting the proper documents to

IVA TOGURI

leave Japan. The last ship leaving for the United States went without her.

Japan attacked the US Navy in Hawaii, and the United States declared war on Japan and Germany. Iva Toguri was stuck in Japan. Her aunt was well now, and Toguri was living with her. But soon neighbors asked her aunt why the enemy was living there. Iva Toguri left her aunt's home.

Toguri tried to find work, but because she was American and did not speak Japanese she could not. Without work, she didn't have money for food. Finally, she found a job as a radio host. The Japanese government told her what to say.

Allied soldiers were stationed on ships within hearing distance of Japanese radio. The Japanese used the radio to spread propaganda, meaning lies. Iva Toguri was one of a group of several female broadcasters, called Tokyo Rose by the Americans. Iva Toguri read messages from the Japanese government to Allied soldiers, many of them American. She told the sailors that American ships were destroyed when they were not and provided other false information to upset the Americans.

After the war was over, Iva Toguri tried to return to the United States and was accused of being the "real" Tokyo Rose. She was arrested and tried for treason. She said she was a loyal American who didn't have a choice but to work for the Japanese. She explained that she had tried to use the tone of her voice to let the sailors know she was lying. For instance, Iva Toguri would announce that the Japanese navy blew up a US battleship. But the battleship was obviously still out there. The men listening on the ship knew it, and the other battleships in communication with the ship knew it.

Some American military personnel said they thought she was funny, and they tuned in every day to listen to her. Others said she was a spy and the things she said hurt them and hurt America.

Iva Toguri was convicted of treason. She was in prison for six years, and one of very few women ever convicted of treason in the United States. Toguri continued to say she was innocent, and President Gerald Ford pardoned her. Eventually the United States gave back her US citizenship.

••FAMOUS SPIES••
••JULIA CHILD••

Most people today recognize the name Julia Child because she wrote a famous book, *Mastering the Art of French Cooking*, and taught half the English-speaking world to cook. But before Julia Child became a successful TV personality, she was Julia McWilliams, a patriotic American who wanted to help in the war effort. At six feet, two inches tall, Child was told she was too tall to join the Women's Army Corps of the United States (**WACs**) or the women's naval branch, the **WAVES**. Instead, Child joined the United States' intelligence service, the OSS.

Julia Child began as a typist in Washington. Intelligent and driven, she was soon transferred to work with the head of the OSS, a general. There were no computers in those days. Child's job was to record the names of all officers in the US spy network, so she had to type thousands of names on small white cards.

JULIA CHILD

Eventually, Julia Child was moved to the OSS Emergency Sea Rescue department. There, she worked with scientists developing shark **repellant**, like mosquito repellant, except for sharks. Sharks were bumping into mines before the mines made contact with enemy ships. The bombs would explode without damaging their targets. Repellant was needed to make the bombs smell and taste bad to the sharks.

Using a variety of ingredients, Julia Child cooked up a formula that worked as a shark repellant. It successfully drove off the sharks and is still used today.

In 1944, Julia Child was posted to the Pacific, playing a vital role in the war effort. She was made chief of OSS Registry. Child had to catalog top secret information about the entire spy network in Asia. Every incoming or outgoing message went through her office. She knew about every spy and what they were doing. She was awarded the Emblem of Meritorious Civilian Service.

Julia Child married a fellow spy, Paul Cushing Child. They moved to Paris, France, where she took cooking classes. She loved to cook and to show people how to cook. With the publication of her cookbook, she became the famous Julia Child, whose books are top sellers even today.

• • IAN FLEMING • •

Before Ian Fleming was a British author, best known for his James Bond novels, he was a spy. During World War II, Ian Fleming worked for Britain's Naval Intelligence Division. He was in charge of two spy units and helped create Operation Goldeneye, a plan for a spy network in Spain.

Ian Fleming was recruited in May 1939. He became the assistant to the director of Naval Intelligence. His code name was 17F. He was soon promoted to commander because of his ability to work with the various sections of the government's wartime espionage departments.

It is said Ian Fleming developed the famous Trout Memo, a kind of how-to manual for spies. For example, it gave instructions for leaving documents with false information on a corpse to fool enemy agents. It also explained how to lure enemy submarines into minefields.

Ian Fleming headed a commando unit with a dangerous mission. They had to go into enemy territory and get hold of documents from German headquarters. All the commandos were trained

IAN FLEMING

in safecracking, lock picking, and unarmed combat.

In August 1944, Target Force, or T-Force, was established. It used intelligence officers to retrieve and guard valuable targets, such as people, equipment, and documents in areas that the Allied Forces had freed. Some of the targets were the secret plans for Germany's long-range rockets and its high-speed submarines. Ian Fleming was responsible for choosing T-Force targets.

Ian Fleming received the King Christian X's Liberty Medal for his role in helping Danish officers escape to England when Denmark was taken over by the Nazis.

After he retired from being a spy, Ian Fleming wrote spy novels, starring James Bond, secret agent 007. The adventures of James Bond were based loosely on Ian Fleming's experiences.

• • HENRY GRAHAM GREENE • •

Henry Graham Greene was an author before he was a spy. He used the name Graham Greene for his writing, and he traveled the world to do research for his novels. He often went to Liberia and other areas of Africa. Many of the countries he visited had weak governments and were filled with political unrest. This gave him ideas for his stories. His travels also gave him information that intelligence services wanted. His sister worked for Britain's MI6, also known as SIS.

HENRY GRAHAM GREENE

She recruited him to become a spy.

Graham Greene continued to write his novels while also working for intelligence organizations. He joined MI6 in 1941. He spent a year and a half as a secret agent in Sierra Leone, a country in Africa. Being a well-known author was a solid cover for his espionage activities. He really was researching his novels, while also secretly collecting information for MI6. He based his book *The Heart of the Matter* on his experiences in Sierra Leone.

He wrote more than twenty-five novels, many with political themes, and he based some, such as *The Quiet American* and *Our Man in Havana*, on his espionage work.

•• MORRIS "MOE" BERG ••

Morris Berg was nicknamed Moe. He was an American baseball player who later became a spy, working for the United States' OSS during World War II.

Moe Berg graduated from Princeton University and Columbia Law School. But he didn't want to be a lawyer. Moe Berg wanted to play professional baseball, and he did, behind home plate. He was a catcher for fifteen years.

Even before World War II, Moe Berg secretly gathered information for the United States. He learned to read and speak Japanese as he prepared for an exhibition baseball game in Japan. One of the greatest baseball players of all time, Babe Ruth, went with him.

MORRIS "MOE" BERG

They arrived in Japan to play baseball in 1934. Moe Berg disguised himself in a kimono. Carrying flowers, he went to a local hospital pretending to visit a patient. Instead, he climbed to the roof of the building and took a panoramic movie of Tokyo. It was illegal for anyone to take photographs or movies of Tokyo at that time. If he had been seen, Japanese authorities could have arrested him. Moe Berg gave his film to a US intelligence organization. It helped the Allies later, when they bombed Tokyo during World War II.

Moe Berg became a spy for the United States' OSS. He was smart, learned languages easily, read multiple newspapers every day, and could disappear into a crowd. He also understood science. For the mission Project Larson, he helped kidnap rocket scientists and bring them to the United States.

Antonio Ferri was an Italian scientist who had worked on the nuclear program for Nazi Germany. The scientist was being hidden somewhere in Italy. Moe Berg had to find him and the scientific documents he held. Not only did Moe Berg find Antonio Ferri, he also translated the scientist's secret documents for the OSS.

Moe Berg traveled to Switzerland to hear a German scientist, Verner Heisenberg, give a lecture about his work. Moe Berg had orders to assassinate the scientist if he was close to developing a nuclear bomb. Berg decided that Heisenberg was not advanced in his research, and so did not kill him.

•• JOSEPHINE BAKER ••

Josephine Baker was an American living in France. She was a popular entertainer who danced for the Folies Bergère. Her act was very popular in Paris.

In September 1939, France declared war on Germany after Germany invaded Poland. The Deuxième Bureau was an intelligence branch of the French military. It recruited Josephine Baker to become a secret agent.

JOSEPHINE BAKER

During the German occupation of France, Josephine Baker, a member of the Free French Forces, entertained troops in Africa and in the Middle East. She was a celebrity and was often invited by the enemy to attend parties where German officers were present. She gathered information about German troop movements at these events and then passed it to the French Resistance and the British.

She moved her family to the south of France, where she continued her spy work. She gathered information about the Germans and wrote it on her sheet music in invisible ink. While performing in other countries, she passed the information to the British.

Josephine Baker pretended she was ill and went to the French colonies in North Africa to recover. While away, she toured Spain to collect information. It was common for the enemy to search foreign travelers, including their personal items. But because Josephine Baker was a celebrity, she was not searched. She hid facts and figures in her underwear.

After the war, Josephine Baker received medals and recognition from the French government for her bravery.

•• ROALD DAHL ••

Before Roald Dahl wrote well-loved children's books, including *Charlie and the Chocolate Factory* and *James and the Giant Peach*, he was a fighter pilot with the Royal Air Force (RAF) and a spy for the British.

Dahl was born in Wales and moved to Africa in 1936 to work for an oil company. In 1939, he joined the United Kingdom's King's African Rifles army. He was put in charge of a troop of local African men who were serving in the colonial army. Later that year, he transferred to the RAF as a fighter pilot. He was given training for a little over seven hours and then told to fly alone. By 1940, he had a squadron under his command and was ready for combat. Roald Dahl fought in several important battles, earning the title of Flying Ace.

In 1942, he was sent home to England because of terrible headaches that caused him to lose consciousness. He wanted to be a flight instructor, but because of his engaging personality and war record, he was sent to work in the British Embassy in the capital of the United States, Washington, DC.

ROALD DAHL

Roald Dahl hated living in Washington while the war raged at home. He felt he wasn't contributing as much as he could. But there was important work to be done in the United States. He was ordered to help change the minds of Americans about getting involved in the war. The American public needed to know that staying out of the war in Europe put the United States in danger.

Roald Dahl started communicating to Americans of all kinds. He wrote stories about his adventures as a Flying Ace, and the *Saturday Evening Post*, a popular magazine, published his stories. This generated interest in Roald Dahl and in England. He talked about his flying experiences in speeches to crowds of people.

Living in Washington, DC, Roald Dahl was close to politicians and other important people. He went to parties and spoke to guests about what he had seen and done in the war. He reported back to Prime Minister Winston Churchill, who wanted to know what President Franklin D. Roosevelt was thinking. Dahl found out by speaking with the people surrounding the president. The information he gathered helped Churchill negotiate American involvement in the war effort.

▶ ▶ ▶ DID YOU KNOW? ◀ ◀ ◀

Freddie Oversteegen was a 14-year-old Dutch girl who became a spy and an ████ armed assassin. Freddie and her older sister bombed bridges and sabotaged railroad lines. They followed enemy soldiers home ██████ and killed them on their doorsteps. No one suspected two schoolgirls on bicycles of killing German soldiers.

•• DOUBLE AGENTS ••

•• MATHILDE CARRÉ ••

Mathilde Carré was a double agent and then a triple agent. Born in France, she went to law school, married a teacher, and moved with him to Africa. After they

MATHILDE CARRÉ

divorced, she returned to Paris in time to witness Nazi Germany invade France. While the French battled the Germans, Mathilde Carré joined the French Army Nurse Corps. After France fell, she went to southern France.

Mathilde Carré soon met a Polish Air Force captain named Roman Czerniawski, who worked for a French-Polish intelligence organization. Mathilde Carré joined the French Resistance and became a leader.

Mathilde Carré and Czerniawski were arrested by the German Abwehr. The Germans interrogated her, threatening to kill her if she didn't cooperate. They offered her a deal. They promised to let her go, and give her money, if she became a double agent. They wanted her to go back and pretend to spy for the Allies, but she would really spy for the Germans. She agreed and continued to operate the radio for Allied intelligence organizations. Part of the deal with the German Abwehr was to give them the names and locations of everyone in the French-Polish spy network. She did, and she continued to work for the Germans.

A spy in the British SOE suspected Mathilde Carré was a double agent for the Nazis. He tricked her into revealing it. When she admitted that he was right, he might have killed her but he did not. Instead the two came up with a plan against the Germans. Carré convinced the German Abwehr to let her go to London and continue her double agent work at SOE headquarters and then report back to Germany. The Abwehr agreed, and when she reached London, she confessed to MI5. SOE questioned her to learn what she knew about Germany's plans, and then they put her in prison until the end of the war.

After the war, the British sent Mathilde Carré to France, where she was convicted of treason and sentenced to death. But instead of being executed, she was jailed for years and then released. Although the French people understood why she became a double agent, they never forgave her. She had caused French Resistance fighters, even those who were friends, to die, and other Allies, too. She was despised for her disloyalty and treason.

Mathilde Carré was called "The Cat," or in French, "La Chatte." Her independence, lack of loyalty, and ability to move through dark places reminded people of a cat.

•• WILLIAM G. SEBOLD, AKA HARRY SAWYER ••

William G. Sebold served in the German army during World War I. In 1922, he moved to America and became a citizen of the United States. He worked in the aircraft industry.

In 1939, he went back to Germany to visit his mother. The Gestapo, or German secret police, confronted him. They ordered him to go back to the United States and spy for Nazi Germany. They threatened his family still living in Germany. They said they would reveal information he had left out of his US citizenship papers if he did not help them. Terrified, Sebold agreed. The Germans sent him to a spy training camp and gave him the code name Harry Sawyer.

WILLIAM G. SEBOLD

Before going back to the United States, William Sebold secretly went to the American Embassy in Germany. He told them about the Gestapo's plans for a spy network in the United States, convinced them he was a loyal American, and offered to help the Allies.

William Sebold was put under the wing of the FBI. He told the agency the identities of the German agents in the spy ring. The FBI set him up in an office in New York City as an engineer.

Nazi agents were fooled into believing his office was a place where they could talk about their activities. They didn't realize the office was **bugged** with hidden microphones and cameras recording their conversations.

The Germans put William Sebold in touch with Fritz Joubert Duquesne, who had been operating as a German spy since World War I. He was also a reporter for the *New York Herald* newspaper. When Duquesne organized a large group of Nazi agents, he reported their names, locations, and activities to William Sebold. He was supposed to send the information to Germany. Instead, William Sebold helped the FBI send false information to Germany.

Thirty-three Nazi spies were captured, and all were found guilty. William Sebold, the double agent, helped bring down a major German espionage ring. He went into the government's **witness protection program**, where he was given a new identity to keep him safe.

•• EDDIE CHAPMAN, AKA FRITZ ••

Edward Arnold Chapman was an English criminal who moved to New York City and worked low-paying jobs that did not support his expensive lifestyle. He moved back to London and began a crime spree. He also became an expert safecracker. He was arrested and sent to an English prison on the Channel Islands. While there, the Germans invaded the Channel Islands, and Eddie Chapman became a spy for Nazi Germany. His German code name was Fritz.

The Germans trained Eddie Chapman in radio communications, explosives, and parachute jumping, as well as other espionage skills. He was sent to Britain to commit acts of sabotage, such as bombing factories. Before he arrived, British intelligence had broken Germany's secret code and knew Germany's plans for Eddie Chapman. As soon as Eddie Chapman arrived in Britain, he

EDDIE CHAPMAN

surrendered to the local police and asked to work for Britain's MI5.

MI5 wanted to put Eddie Chapman to work right away. They planned to send him back to Germany to spy for them. But first they had to make sure the Nazis would trust him, so they created "fake sabotage," and reports about it. Eddie Chapman went to Germany and claimed he had completed his sabotage missions. To make his story even more believable, MI5 sent out fake newspaper articles about the sabotage. The Nazis believed Eddie Chapman was their loyal spy.

Eventually they sent Eddie Chapman back to Britain to report on damage from German aircraft bombings. Working with MI5, he gave the Germans false information. Eddie Chapman reported that the bombs were hitting their targets in the heart of London, when they were not. They were being dropped in a much less populated area, doing less damage and killing fewer people. The Germans believed his reports and never corrected their aim. Eddie Chapman saved thousands of British civilian lives.

•• JUAN PUJOL GARCÍA, AKA GARBO ••

Juan Pujol García was born in Spain and worked for the Spanish government. He pretended to be pro-Nazi, but both he and his wife hated the Nazi government in Germany. They contacted the Allies and offered to spy for them, but both American and British intelligence organizations rejected them. Juan Pujol García decided to fool the Nazis into believing he was a Nazi spy and then go to the Allies and offer himself as a double agent.

JUAN PUJOL GARCÍA

The Nazis gave him a code name and a mission. He was Alaric, and they ordered him to spy for them in Britain. Instead of going to Britain, he and his wife secretly went to Lisbon, Portugal. There, Juan Pujol García used magazines, train timetables, tourist guides, newsreels, and maps to create fake reports about British life. He also created a fake spy network that the Nazis believed was real. They called the network Arabal.

After one of García's reports had the Germans searching for British soldiers and tanks that didn't exist, the British realized they had someone giving false information to the Nazis and that this could be useful. The Allies recruited García and moved him and his family to Britain.

The British gave him the code name Garbo. By the time they started working together, the Germans were paying for twenty-seven agents that didn't exist. The Germans were so overwhelmed with all the information the fake agents were passing, they stopped recruiting agents in Britain.

Juan Pujol García was important to **Operation Fortitude**. He convinced the Germans that the Allied Normandy invasion was coming in through the south of France.

The Nazis never realized Juan Pujol García was a double agent. He received medals of honor from both the Allies and the Germans.

► ESPIONAGE BY THE NUMBERS ◄

There were 115 ▮▮▮ agents working for the Nazis against the British. All but one of them was identified and caught.

CHAPTER 6

CODE BREAKERS

COMMUNICATION THAT MUST BE KEPT secret is encrypted. This was true during World War II and is still the case today. When information is encrypted, it is translated into a secret coded message that can only be read if the person receiving it knows how to convert it into its original form.

During the war, tens of thousands of people worked for the Allies to crack the codes that the enemy used to communicate secrets. Cracking enemy codes meant understanding enemy communications about battle plans, troop positions, and other important information. When this happened, and the enemies' secret plans were revealed, the Allies moved closer to victory. Here are some of the people, places, and machines that helped the Allied Forces break the codes.

•• THE ENIGMA MACHINE ••

The word "enigma" means "riddle." The Germans used a small machine called the **Enigma** to communicate secret information. The Enigma looked like a typewriter with extra buttons. During the war, there were Enigma machines in offices, battlefields, ships, and submarines.

A person sending information would type on the Enigma machine, like on a computer today. Inside the machine, cylinders and wheels scrambled the letters and words into a secret coded message. The person who received the message could only unscramble it if they had an Enigma machine, as well as the key to set the cylinders and wheels to the same position as the sender's machine.

The machine's settings were changed daily, so the codes were completely different every day.

THE ENIGMA MACHINE

One of the most important breakthroughs in the war was when the Allies decoded, or broke the code of, the Enigma machine.

In many different countries, people worked in secret, trying to figure out the Enigma. A Polish mathematician broke the code, while a French spy stole the cipher, or secret key.

The British also broke Enigma's code, which meant they could read Nazi Germany's secret messages. It was a great achievement, but the British had to keep it a secret. If the Germans realized their communications were no longer secret, they would change the method of coding their messages.

Keeping this secret meant that when the British learned the Germans planned to bomb British cities, the residents were not told to leave. If the government had warned people to leave these cities, then the Germans would have realized the British had broken the German code and were reading their secret messages. This meant allowing innocent citizens to be bombed, when instead they could have been evacuated and their lives saved. It was the terrible price that the British paid in exchange for defeating the enemy sooner. If the code had not been broken, or if Germany changed the code, years might have been added to the war, and many more lives would have been lost.

• • BLETCHLEY PARK • •

Bletchley Park was an estate located in the center of England. It was bought by a high-ranking admiral as an ideal location for future employees, due to its central location. It was near the railway line between two college towns, Oxford and Cambridge. That was important for recruiting the brightest minds in England.

The manor was set up to house the British Government Code and Cypher School, which was created to break the secret messages being used by the enemy.

They created cover names for the covert operations taking place in the house. They called it the London Signals Intelligence Centre and Government Communication Headquarters.

Code breakers at Bletchley Park created the first programmable computer, called Colossus. They worked on figuring out a way to understand the Enigma machine. This was essential to any victory for the Allies.

People who study language (called linguists), chess champions, and mathematicians, along with others who were good at solving crossword puzzles, were sent to work on cryptology there. In fact, the *Daily Telegraph*, an English newspaper, was asked by the government to create a crossword competition. The smartest people were asked to join the war effort at Bletchley.

Alan Turing was a British mathematician, **cryptanalyst**, and logician. He was also a leader in the new field of computer science. He joined the team at Bletchley, where he worked on decoding the German ciphers. His work to crack the code was important in helping shorten the war.

Over 10,000 people worked in total secrecy at the estate. Since many men were sent to battlefields, many women with college degrees were given opportunities to help with the project.

Bletchley Park and its workers were called Ultra by British Military Intelligence. The word "Ultra" became commonly used by the Allies when they were talking about information that was most secret.

▶ ▶ ▶ DID YOU KNOW? ◀ ◀ ◀

Life was so secret at ▓▓▓▓Bletchley Park that everyone had to sign an official document saying they would not talk. They were told, "Do not talk at meals. ▓▓Do not talk in the transport. Do not talk traveling. Do not talk in the billet. Do not ▓▓▓▓talk by your own fireside. Be careful."

•• JAPANESE PURPLE MACHINE ••

The Japanese used a machine that scrambled its secret communications into coded messages so they could not be read. The first machine they used was called the Red Machine, and the Americans broke the code early on. Starting in 1938, their new machine was the Purple Machine. The Americans were quick to break this code, too. They gave the secret information, or intelligence, revealed by Japan's codes a special name: Magic.

Before the attack on Pearl Harbor, the United States was decoding and translating all messages

THE PURPLE MACHINE

going back and forth between the Japanese government and its embassy in Hawaii. A secret message was sent by the Japanese government saying that Japan planned to break off talks with the United States. This was considered an act of war, and the US government needed to see this intelligence. However, even though the message was decoded and translated, it was not seen in time. In fact, the White House did not see the message until months after the attack.

As partners in the war against the Allied Forces, Japan and Nazi Germany shared military information. Fortunately for the Allies, a Japanese general sent Hitler's military plans to Tokyo. He communicated often with Tokyo using Purple Machines. Without either Japan or Germany knowing it, the Americans decoded all of the general's messages and learned Hitler's plans before they were carried out.

The Soviet Union also broke the Purple code. The Japanese didn't learn that their codes had been broken until after the end of World War II.

•• CODE TALKERS ••

The American military had hundreds of Native American code talkers, military personnel who communicated secretly using Native American languages unknown to most of the world. They were especially valuable on the front lines. They let commanding officers transmit battle orders in secret.

Many Native American languages were not taught in school and were little known. This made the languages perfect for encoding communications. There were two ways of doing this: Secret messages substituted a Native American word for each of the twenty-six letters of the English alphabet, or the entire message was translated directly into a Native American language. Either way, it was a nearly unbreakable code. The encrypted message could be delivered without the enemy understanding it.

For the second method, a code talker had to be with each officer sending and receiving a secret message. On the sending side, the code talker took the message in English and encrypted it. This meant they translated it into the coded message using their Native American language, then spoke the words of the encrypted message into a radio or portable phone. On the receiving side, another code talker listened by radio or portable phone. They deciphered the secret message, or translated it, and told their commanding officer the original English message. If it was a secret battle plan, and the enemy had listened to it, they didn't understand it.

The German military remembered that the Americans used code talkers during World War I. To prepare for World War II, Nazi Germany sent a team of thirty scientists to America to study Native American languages. They wanted to learn how to use them to code messages. The Germans found it was impossible. There were too many tribal languages, and each language differed by region.

Fourteen Comanche code talkers created a code of over a hundred words to be used to communicate messages for the Allied Invasion of Normandy, or D-Day. Sometimes there was no direct translation for a word, so the Comanches made creative substitutions. The word "tank" became the Comanche word for "turtle" and a bomber became a "pregnant airplane."

Navajo code talkers sent and received over six hundred messages during the Battle of Iwo Jima in the Pacific. It was a key battle that the Allied Forces won in large part because of six code talkers. A top officer said, "Were it not for the Navajos, the Marines would never have taken Iwo Jima."

> **► ESPIONAGE BY THE NUMBERS ◄**
>
> During World War II, the US Marine Corps recruited 400 to 500 ▓▓▓▓ Native Americans to ▓▓▓▓ transmit secret ▓▓▓ military messages.

CONCLUSION

<u>SPIES TODAY</u>

THE CREATIVITY AND BRAVERY OF WORLD War II spies are legendary, but did you know spies live among us today?

Spies are everywhere, in every country. Foreign spies live in cities and towns all over the United States, watching and then reporting to their agency handlers. American spies live in foreign countries doing the same thing. They report what they see and hear. Spies sit in marketplaces, attend parties, and hang around college campuses. They let the home government know the political and economic climate of both friendly and unfriendly nations. The intelligence that spies collect is important to government operations.

In the United States, experts ███ estimate there are 100,000 ███ secret agents working for sixty to eighty nations—all spying on ███ America.

There are all types of spies in the world today. MI5 and MI6 are still active in the United Kingdom. The United States' OSS was replaced by the CIA. When the Soviet Union collapsed, Russia became an independent country, and its intelligence services are the Foreign Intelligence Service and Federal Security Service. Germany has the Federal Intelligence Service, and France has the Directorate-General for External Security.

Spies make a lot of money stealing valuable information and selling it. Sometimes spies steal a company's designs for a new invention and sell them to a competitor. There are **cyber** spies who go online and steal passwords and private information from individuals and companies. Then they sell it to criminals, who use stolen identities for many illegal activities, including stealing money. Spies in banking and financial jobs also gather secret information and sell it. The people or companies buying this information use it illegally. For instance, they might buy and sell stocks and make large amounts of money.

In World War II, some spies spread propaganda. They still do this today. Spies can be found all over social media, planting fake stories, stirring up public unrest, and swaying political elections.

There are countless numbers of spies out there. If you pay close attention, you may spot one yourself!

GLOSSARY

ABWEHR: the German spy organization.

AGENT: a person who acts on behalf of another person or group.

ALLIED FORCES: a group of nations that worked together against the Axis Powers. Major Allied nations included Great Britain, France, the United States, and the Soviet Union. Countries joined the group at different times.

ASSASSINATE: to kill a target for political or other reasons.

AXIS POWERS: a group of nations that worked together against the Allied Forces. Major Axis nations included Germany, Italy, and Japan.

BUGGED: when a device is hidden to record a person speaking without the person knowing.

CIPHER: writing that is disguised or secret, a code.

CIVILIAN: a person who is not part of the police or military.

COAL GRENADES: hollowed-out pieces of iron made to look like lumps of coal and filled with explosives.

CODE: a system of translating information into another form to communicate it, sometimes secretly.

CODE BREAKER: a person working to take a coded, or encrypted, message and change it back to its original form.

CODE TALKER: a person who uses their knowledge of little-known languages to communicate secretly.

COMMUNISM: a political theory that promotes total public ownership of all property.

CONCENTRATION CAMP: a place where people are kept against their will during a war, often in very poor conditions.

COURIER: messenger.

CRYPTANALYST: an expert in deciphering or translating coded messages.

CRYPTOLOGY: the study of codes and how to solve them.

CYBER: related to computers.

D-DAY: code name for the Invasion of Normandy, when the Allied Forces invaded German-occupied France.

DECIPHER: to translate a message written in secret code.

DOUBLE CROSS: when a secret agent changes from working as a spy for group A, getting information about group B, to working as a spy for group B, getting information about group A, and does this without telling group A. This can involve a double agent sending false information to his or her former spy agency.

ENIGMA: a device that translated messages into code, or another form, to keep them secret.

ESPIONAGE: the practice of spying or of using spies.

FASCIST: when a dictator and/or one political party totally controls a country.

GESTAPO: the Nazi secret police.

HANDLER: a person who is in charge of someone else, often a spy.

INTELLIGENCE: the information that a spy gathers.

INTRIGUE: secret plans and activities.

LIAISON: a person who acts as a link between two people or groups to carry messages or physical objects.

LIMPET MINE: a small, magnetic bomb that attaches to a metal surface underwater.

MI5: a British spy organization.

MI6: a British spy organization.

MORSE CODE: a method of using dots and dashes to send messages.

NAZI: someone who was part of the fascist National Socialist German Workers' Party headed by Adolf Hitler.

NKVD (People's Commissariat for Internal Affairs): the Soviet Union's spy agency.

OPERATION FORTITUDE: the code name for a successful Allied mission to fool Nazi Germany into believing the Allied invasion of German-occupied Europe would not take place at Normandy, France.

OSS (Office of Strategic Services): the US spy agency organized during World War II. It later became the CIA (Central Intelligence Agency).

POLISH INTELLIGENCE: the official spy organization of Poland.

PRISONER-OF-WAR CAMP: a place where a military keeps enemy soldiers after capturing them during a war.

RECRUIT: to find the right people for an organization and convince them to join.

REPARATIONS: payment to an individual, group, or nation as a sort of punishment.

REPELLANT: a substance that makes one thing move away from another.

RESISTANCE: a group secretly fighting against rulers.

RSHA (Reich Main Security Office): a spy agency helping the Gestapo, the Nazi secret police.

SABOTAGE: to act secretly to destroy or damage something.

SOE (Special Operations Executive): the British spy agency organized during World War II.

SOVIET UNION: the name for Russia after revolutions destroyed both the ruling royal family and the new democratic government formed to replace it.

SPECIAL TRAINING SCHOOL 103: a school in Canada that taught people to become spies for the Allied Forces.

TRANSMITTER: a device that sends out information using electromagnetic waves.

TREATY OF VERSAILLES: the 1919 peace agreement between Germany and the Allied Powers of Britain, France, Italy, the United States, and the Soviet Union, ending World War I.

UNARMED COMBAT: fighting without weapons.

UNDERGROUND: a group or movement organized secretly to fight against the current government or rulers.

WACS: Women's Army Corps, a women's branch of the US Army.

WAVES: part of the US Naval Reserve, a women's branch of the Navy.

WITNESS PROTECTION PROGRAM: a way for the US government to hide people who give dangerous information to the US government, giving the people new identities and places to live.

RESOURCES

•• BOOKS ABOUT ESPIONAGE ••

Mundy, Liza. *Code Girls: The True Story of the American Women Who Secretly Broke Codes in World War II*, Young Readers Edition. New York: Little, Brown and Company, 2018.

Olson, Lynne. *Madame Fourcade's Secret War: The Daring Young Woman Who Led France's Largest Spy Network against Hitler*. New York: Random House, 2019.

Pearson, Judith. *The Wolves at the Door: The True Story of America's Greatest Female Spy*. New York: Lyons Publishing, 2009.

Rose, Sarah. *D-Day Girls: The Spies Who Armed the Resistance, Sabotaged the Nazis, and Helped Win World War II*. New York: Crown Publishing Group, 2019.

Swanson, Jennifer, and Kevin O'Malley. *Spies, Lies, and Disguise: The Daring Tricks and Deeds that Won World War II*. New York: Bloomsbury Children's Books, 2019.

•• WEBSITES ABOUT ESPIONAGE ••

Mundy, Liza. "Female Spies and Their Secrets." *The Atlantic,* June 2019. www.theatlantic.com/magazine/archive/2019/06/female -spies-world-war-ii/588058/.

Nix, Elizabeth. "6 People You Didn't Know Were WWII Spies." *History.com*, A&E Television Networks, 11 Nov. 2014. www.history.com/news/6-people-you-didnt-know-were-wwii-spies.

"Roald Dahl." *About Roald Dahl*, www.roalddahl.com/roald-dahl.

Roos, Dave. "World War II's 'Most Dangerous' Allied Spy Was a Woman with a Wooden Leg." *History.com*, A&E Television Networks, 30 May 2018. www.history.com/news/female-allied-spy-world-war-2-wooden-leg.

"Spy Gadgets of World War II: Historical Spotlight: News." *Wargaming*, wargaming.com/en/news/spy_gadgets/.

"World War II." *Ducksters Education Site*. www.ducksters.com/history/world_war_ii/spies_and_secret_agents_of_ww2.php.

"World War II Spy School." *Smithsonian Channel*, www.smithsonianchannel.com/shows/world-war-ii-spy-school/0/3416231.

• • MONUMENTS FOR SPIES • •

Aleutian Islands World War II National Historic Area, Alaska • https://www.nps.gov/aleu/index.htm

Catoctin Mountain Park, Fredericksburg, Maryland • https://www.nps.gov/cato/learn/historyculture/wwii.htm

Prince William Forest Park, Triangle, Virginia • https://www.nps.gov/prwi/learn/historyculture/oss.htm

Radar Station B-71: Redwood National Park • https://www.nps.gov/places/redwoodradarstation.htm

Wading River Radio Station (U.S. National Park Service) • https://
www.nps.gov/places/wading-river-radio-station.htm

• • MUSEUMS • •

Bletchley Park, Milton Keynes, United Kingdom •
https://bletchleypark.org.uk/

German Spy Museum, Berlin, Germany • https://www.deutsches
-spionagemuseum.de/en/

International Spy Museum, Washington, DC •
https://www.spymuseum.org/

KGB Espionage Museum, New York, New York •
https://kgbespionagemuseum.org/

National Cryptologic Museum, Fort Meade, Maryland •
https://www.nsa.gov/about/cryptologic-heritage/museum/

Spyscape, New York, New York • https://spyscape.com/

BIBLIOGRAPHY

"5 Fascinating Facts About Josephine Baker." *Mental Floss*, 3 June 2019. mentalfloss.com/article/23148/5-things-you-didnt-know-about-josephine-baker.

"Agent Garbo." MI5 Security Service. www.mi5.gov.uk/agent-garbo.

Alberto-Perez. "How the U.S. Cracked Japan's 'Purple Encryption Machine' at the Dawn of World War II." *io9*, 16 Dec. 2015. io9.gizmodo.com/how-the-u-s -cracked-japans-purple-encryption-machine-458385664.

Alderson, Andrew. "Roald Dahl Was a Real-Life James Bond Style Spy, New Book Reveals." *The Telegraph*, Telegraph Media Group, 7 Aug. 2010. www.telegraph .co.uk/culture/books/booknews/7931835/Roald-Dahl-was-a-real-life-James -Bond-style-spy-new-book-reveals.html.

"Biography: The Official Site of Josephine Baker." *Josephine Baker*. www.cmgww .com/stars/baker/about/biography/.

Bradsher, Greg. "A Time to Act: The Beginning of the Fritz Kolbe Story, 1900–1943." *Prologue Magazine*, National Archives and Records Administration, Spring 2002, 34(1). www.archives.gov/publications/prologue/2002/spring /fritz-kolbe-1.html.

Carter, Ilise. "Christine Granville, World War II Special Agent." *Mental Floss*, 29 Mar. 2018. mentalfloss.com/article/74271/retrobituaries-christine-granville -wwii-special-agent.

Copeland, B. J. "Ultra." *Encyclopædia Britannica*, Encyclopædia Britannica, Inc. www.britannica.com/topic/Ultra-Allied-intelligence-project.

"D-Day: June 6, 1944: The United States Army." The United States Army. www.army.mil/d-day/.

"Duquesne Spy Ring." FBI, 18 May 2016. www.fbi.gov/history/famous-cases /duquesne-spy-ring.

"Eddie Chapman: MI5: The Security Service." MI5 Security Service. www .mi5.gov.uk/eddie-chapman.

Frost, Natasha. "Julia Child's Spy Days Included Work on a Shark Repellent." *History.com*, A&E Television Networks, 30 May 2018. www.history.com/news /julia-child-oss-spy-wwii-shark-repellent.

Goldstein, Richard. "Eddie Chapman, 83, Safecracker and Spy." *The New York Times*, 20 Dec. 1997. www.nytimes.com/1997/12/20/world/eddie-chapman-83 -safecracker-and-spy.html.

"Graham Greene's FBI File." *Spy Culture*, 23 May 2016. www.spyculture.com /graham-greenes-fbi-file/.

Hays, Jeffrey. "American Strategy in World War II, Supply Lines, Ships, Codes and Spies." *Facts and Details,* Nov. 2013. factsanddetails.com/asian/ca67 /sub428/item2527.html.

Hemmings, Jay. "Spy Once, Live Twice—a Legendary Double-Agent Faked His Death For 36 Years." *War History Online*, 13 Mar. 2019. www.warhistoryonline .com/instant-articles/juan-pujol-garcia.html.

"Heroines of WW2: The Special Operations Executive." *The Gazette*, www .thegazette.co.uk/all-notices/content/100273.

Hines, Nickolaus. "How William Sebold Took Down the Largest Nazis' Spy Ring in U.S. History." *All That's Interesting*, 5 Feb. 2018. allthatsinteresting.com /duquesne-spy-ring-william-sebold.

History.com Editors. "World War II." *History.com*, A&E Television Networks, 29 Oct. 2009. www.history.com/topics/world-war-ii/world-war-ii-history.

Holt, Bryant. "Juan Pujol Garcia: The Greatest Spy of World War II." *Innovative History | 3 Minute History Videos*, 16 Jan. 2018. innovativehistory.com/ih-blog /juan-pujol-garcia-greatest-spy-of-world-war-ii.

"Ian Fleming: The Man Behind the Most Famous Spy." Central Intelligence Agency, 29 May 2018. www.cia.gov/news-information/featured-story-archive /2018-featured-story-archive/ian-fleming-the-man-behind-the-most-famous -spy.html.

"Ignatz Theodor Griebl." Revolvy, LLC. www.revolvy.com/page/Ignatz-Theodor -Griebl.

Jarvis, Erika. "Five Badass Female Spies Who Deserve Their Own World War II Movie." *Vanity Fair*, 23 Nov. 2016. www.vanityfair.com/hollywood/2016/11 /allied-world-war-2-female-spy-movies.

"Julia Child Cooked Up Double Life as Spy." *NBCNews.com*, NBCUniversal News Group, 14 Aug. 2008. www.nbcnews.com/id/26186498/ns/us_news-security/t /julia-child-cooked-double-life-spy.

Klein, Christopher. "When Roald Dahl Spied on the United States." *History.com*, A&E Television Networks, 14 Sept. 2016. www.history.com/news/when-roald -dahl-spied-on-the-united-states.

Leith, Sam. "The Spy Who Loved: The Secrets and Lives of Christine Granville by Clare Mulley—Review." *The Guardian*, Guardian News and Media, 3 Aug. 2012. www.theguardian.com/books/2012/aug/03/spy-loved-granville-mulley -review.

Little, Becky. "The WWII Spy Who Faked His Death for 36 Years." *History.com*, A&E Television Networks, 1 June 2018. www.history.com/news/spy-double -agent-death-hoax-world-war-2.

"Mathilde Carré." Revolvy, LLC. www.revolvy.com/page/Mathilde-Carré.

Mawer, Simon. "Special Agents: The Women of SOE." *The Paris Review*, 21 May 2012. www.theparisreview.org/blog/2012/05/21/special-agents-the-women-of-soe/.

"Morris 'Moe' Berg." *Atomic Heritage Foundation*. www.atomicheritage.org /profile/morris-moe-berg-1.

Mortimer, Gavin. "The Adventures of Mutt and Jeff." *HistoryNet*, HistoryNet, Apr. 2011. www.historynet.com/adventures-mutt-jeff.htm.

Mundy, Liza. "The Secret History of the Female Code Breakers Who Helped Defeat the Nazis." *POLITICO Magazine*, 10 Oct. 2017. www.politico.com /magazine/story/2017/10/10/the-secret-history-of-the-women-code-breakers -who-helped-defeat-the-nazis-215694.

Nix, Elizabeth. "6 People You Didn't Know Were WWII Spies." *History.com*, A&E Television Networks, 11 Nov. 2014.www.history.com/news/6-people-you-didnt -know-were-wwii-spies.

Noe, Rain. "Escape Kits: Real-Life British Spy Gadgets from World War II." *Core77*, 8 Jan. 2018. www.core77.com/posts/71473/Escape-Kits-Real-Life -British-Spy-Gadgets-from-World-War-II.

Nye, David. "6 of the Wildest Top Secret Spy Missions of World War II." *Business Insider*, 20 Aug. 2015. www.businessinsider.com/6-of-the-wildest-top-secret -spy-missions-of-world-war-ii-2015-8.

"Operatives, Spies and Saboteurs: The Unknown Story of the Men and Women of World War II's OSS." Central Intelligence Agency, 26 June 2008. www.cia .gov/library/center-for-the-study-of-intelligence/csi-publications/csi-studies /studies/vol49no1/html_files/the_unknown_story_9.html.

"Pearl Harbor Spy." FBI, 18 May 2016. www.fbi.gov/history/famous-cases/pearl -harbor-spy.

"Polish Intelligence During World War II." *Poland and Poles in the Second World War*. ww2.pl/polish-intelligence-during-world-war-ii/.

Pop, Cassie. "How Poland Proved Vital to the Allied War Effort in World War Two." *History Hit*, 12 Sept. 2018. www.historyhit.com/how-poland-proved-vital -to-allied-war-effort-in-world-war-two/.

"Richard Sorge." HistoryofSpies.com, 29 Dec. 2017. historyofspies.com /richard-sorge/.

Roig-Franzia, Manuel. "The Strange Life and Death of Moe Berg, the Baseball Catcher Who Became a Spy." *The Washington Post*, 7 June 2019. www .washingtonpost.com/lifestyle/style/the-strange-life-and-death-of-moe-berg -the-baseball-catcher-who-became-a-spy/2019/06/06/37f96782-82d6-11e9-933d -7501070ee669_story.html.

Roos, Dave. "World War II's 'Most Dangerous' Allied Spy Was a Woman with a Wooden Leg." *History.com*, A&E Television Networks, 30 May 2018. www .history.com/news/female-allied-spy-world-war-2-wooden-leg.

Sebba, Anne. "The Forgotten Women of the French Resistance." *The Telegraph*, Telegraph Media Group, 11 July 2016. www.telegraph.co.uk/books/what-to-read /the-forgotten-women-of-the-french-resistance.

Siegphyl. "Crafty Gadgets and Famous Spies of WWII." *War History Online*, 5 Feb. 2015. www.warhistoryonline.com/war-articles/crafty-gadgets-tricks -famous-wwii-spies.html.

Simner, Mark. "Agent Zigzag: From Criminal to Double Agent." *WWII Nation*. ww2nation.com/agent-zigzag-from-criminal-to-double-agent-the-true -wartime-adventures-of-eddie-chapman/.

SOFREP. "OSS Weapons Ingenuity: The Secret Gear of America's WWII Spies." *NEWSREP*, 11 Jan. 2018. thenewsrep.com/97864/oss-weapons-ingenuity -secret-gear-americas-wwii-spies-2/.

"Spy Gadgets of World War II: Historical Spotlight: News." *Wargaming*. wargaming.com/en/news/spy_gadgets/.

Tremain, David. "Mathilde Carré: The Second World War's 'Exceedingly Dangerous Woman.'" *The History Press*. www.thehistorypress.co.uk/articles /mathilde-carré-the-second-world-war-s-exceedingly-dangerous-woman/.

Trueman, C. N. "The Phoney War." *History Learning Site,* 20 Apr. 2015. www .historylearningsite.co.uk/world-war-two/world-war-two-in-western-europe /the-phoney-war/.

Wei-Haas, Maya. "How the American Women Codebreakers of WWII Helped Win the War." *Smithsonian.com*, Smithsonian Institution, 5 Oct. 2017. www .smithsonianmag.com/history/how-women-codebreakers-wwii-helped-win -war-180965058/.

Winterbotham, F. W. *The Ultra Secret.* Dell, 15 Nov. 1975.

"World War II Spy School." Smithsonian Channel. https://www .smithsonianchannel.com/shows/world-war-ii-spy-school/0/3416231.

Yiu, Melody. *Graham Greene Biography.* greeneland.tripod.com/bio.htm.

INDEX

A

Abwehr, 8, 11, 23–24, 27, 60–62
Allied Forces, x. *See also*
    France; Great Britain;
    Soviet Union; United
    States
Axis Powers, x. *See also*
    Germany; Japan

B

Baker, Josephine, 89–90
Battles, 32–34
    Battle of Iwo Jima, 113–114
    Battle of Midway, 13–14
    D-Day, 33, 34–36
Berg, Morris "Moe," 87–89
Bletchley Park, 107–109
Bombs, 39–40, 45–46, 49–50
Bugging, 98

C

Cameras, 44
Camp X, 30–32
Carré, Mathilde, 93–96
Chapman, Eddie (Fritz),
    98–100
Child, Julia, 81–83
Ciphers, 29

Clothing, 53–55
Coal grenades, 39–40
Codes and code breaking,
    26, 29, 32, 34, 104–105
    Bletchley Park, 107–109
    code talkers, 26, 33–34,
        111–114
    Enigma machine, 105–107
    Morse code, 43
    Purple Machine, 110–111
Communications equipment,
    42–45
Concentration camps, 65
    Couriers, 74
    Cryptanalysts, 109
    Cryptology, 58
Cyber spies, 116–117
Czerniawski, Roman, 94

D

Dahl, Roald, 91–93
Dasch, George, 50
D-Day, 33, 34–36
Deciphering, 34. *See also* Codes
    and code breaking
Detection-escaping tools, 52–53
Double agents, 11, 93–103
Double Cross System, 59
Duquesne, Fritz Joubert, 98

E

Enigma machine, 105–107

F

Fascism, 2
Ferri, Antonio, 88
Fleming, Ian, 83–85
Footprints, 47–48
France
    spies in, 9, 62–63, 116
    World War II, 3–5
French Resistance Movement,
        62–63
Fritz (Eddie Chapman), 98–100

G

García, Juan Pujol (Garbo),
        101–103
Germany
    spies in, 8, 11–12,
        60–62, 116
    World War I, 2–3
    World War II, 3–7
Gestapo, 12, 61
Glad, Tor (Mutt and Jeff),
        34–35, 74–75
Granville, Christine (Maria
        Krystyna Janina
        Starbek), 76–78
Great Britain
    spies in, 7–9, 57–59, 65, 116
    World War II, 3–5, 7
Great Depression, 15–16

Greene, Henry Graham, 85–86
Guns, 40–41

H

Hall, Virginia, 67–69
Heisenberg, Verner, 88–89
Hitler, Adolf, 2–3
Hydra, 32

I

Identity documents, 52
Immigrants, 8, 21–23
Intelligence, 7, 29
Invisible ink, 45
Isolationism, 15–16
Iwo Jima, Battle of, 113–114

J

Japan, 12–15

K

Kolbe, Fritz (George Wood),
        72–74
Kuehn, Bernard Julius Otto,
        14, 37

L

League of Nations, 15
Liaisons, 68
Limpet mines, 45–46

M

Maps, 50–51
Midway, Battle of, 13–14
Military Intelligence Section
     5 (MI5), 57–58, 59, 60
Military Intelligence Section
     6 (MI6), 27, 58
Moe, John (Mutt and Jeff),
     34–35, 74–75
Morse code, 43
Mutt and Jeff, 34–35, 74–75

N

Native Americans, 26, 33–34,
     111–114
Nazis, 2–3
NKVD (People's Commissariat
     for Internal Affairs),
     11, 63–64
Normandy, Invasion of,
     33, 34–36

O

Occupied territories, 8–9
Office of Strategic Services
     (OSS), 24–25, 59–60
Operation Fortitude, 102
Oversteegen, Freddie, 93

P

Pacific Ocean
     spies in, 14–15
     World War II, 12–14

Pearl Harbor, 12, 36–37
People's Commissariat for
     Internal Affairs (NKVD),
     11, 63–64
Poison, 52–53
Poland
     spies in, 10, 64–65
     World War II, 3–4, 6
Polish Intelligence, 10, 64–65
Prisoner-of-war camps, 50–51
Propaganda, 14–15, 27–28, 117
Purple Machine, 110–111

R

Radio transmitters, 43
Ramsay (Richard Sorge),
     69–72
Recruitment, 21–27
Reich Main Security Office
     (RSHA), 60–62
Reparations, 2
Resistance fighters, 6,
     9–11. *See also* French
     Resistance Movement
Royal Air Force (RAF)
     Photographic
     Reconnaissance Unit, 58
Russia, 116. *See also* Soviet
     Union

S

Sabotage, 9, 45–50
Sawyer, Harry (William G.
     Sebold), 96–98

Schools, for spies, 30–32
Sebold, William G. (Harry
      Sawyer), 96–98
Secret agents, 1. *See also* Spies
Secret Intelligence Service
      (SIS). *See* Military
      Intelligence Section
      6 (MI6)
Shark repellant, 82
Sorge, Richard (Ramsay),
      69–72
Soviet Union
   spies in, 11, 63–64
   World War II, 3–6
Special Operations Executive
      (SOE), 25, 57, 65
Special Training School
      103, 30–32
Spies
   female, 55
   jobs of, 27–29
   modern, 115–117
   qualifications of, 19–21
   recruitment of, 21–27
   schools for, 30–32
Starbek, Maria Krystyna Janina
      (Christine Granville),
      76–78

T
Toguri, Iva (Tokyo Rose), 15,
      78–80
Treaty of Versailles, 2, 60
Trout Memo, 84
Turing, Alan, 109

U
Underwater breathing devices,
      46–47
United States
   spies in, 17–18, 59–60, 116
   World War II, 5, 12–13, 15–17

W
Weapons, 39–41
Wilson, Woodrow, 15
Witness protection program, 98
Wood, George (Fritz Kolbe),
      72–74
World War I, 2–3
World War II, x–xi, 3–7

Y
Yoshikawa, Takeo, 14, 37

ACKNOWLEDGMENTS

As the niece and wife of veterans, I realize the necessity of espionage in times of war. I remember the stories my mother told of my uncle at Pearl Harbor, another at Iwo Jima on that infamous day, or my two other uncles participating in D-Day when they were barely out of their teens.

I know of assorted cousins hiding in the forest of Poland as the Resistance fighters I learned about, and I realized that war touches us both directly and indirectly.

Spies were essential in bringing all my relatives home from the battlefields. Without their selfless contribution, my father would not have been liberated from a concentration camp, and my freedom-fighting cousins would have perished from lack of support.

Without the code talkers at Iwo Jima, or Moe Berg taking forbidden pictures of Tokyo, my uncles might not have survived warfare in the Pacific.

Operation Fortitude might have saved the lives of my other uncles as they slogged on the beaches of Normandy. The false information sent to the Germans meant the Allies faced a weaker and divided force.

Without these spies and their bravery and selfless devotion, the world could have looked very different today.

Special thanks to Callisto Media for giving me this project. Heartfelt gratitude to Joe Cho and Kristen Depken for working hand-in-hand with me to bring forth this book.

Brittney Leigh Bass, I couldn't accomplish much without your help and expertise.

Shout-out to my brilliant brother, who always knows the answers to my questions.

My children and grandchildren are always there with both encouragement and support.

Last, to the courageous men and women, including my husband and the rest of my family, who braved the battlefields, on the front lines or clandestinely, to keep the world a safer place.

Carole P. Roman
Hicksville, NY, 2019

ABOUT THE AUTHOR

CAROLE P. ROMAN is the award-winning author of over fifty children's books. Whether it's pirates, princesses, or discovering the world around us, her books have enchanted educators, parents, and her diverse audience of children. She hosts a blog radio program called Indie Authors Roundtable and is one of the founders of the magazine *Indie Authors Monthly*. She's been interviewed twice by *Forbes*. Carole has coauthored two self-help books: *Navigating Indieworld: A Beginners Guide to Self-Publishing and Marketing Your Book* with Julie A. Gerber, and *Marketing Indieworld* with both Julie A. Gerber and Angela Hausman. She published *Mindfulness for Kids* with J. Robin Albertson-Wren and *The Big Book of Silly Jokes for Kids: 800+ Jokes!* She writes adult fiction under the name Brit Lunden and is currently helping to create an anthology with her mythical town of Bulwark, Georgia, with a group of indie authors. She lives on Long Island near her children and grandchildren.

Her work includes:

Captain No Beard

If You Were Me and Lived in: Cultural

If You Were Me and Lived in: Historical

Nursery series

Oh Susannah (early reader and coloring book)

Mindfulness for Kids, with coauthor J. Robin Albertson-Wren

The Big Book of Silly Jokes for Kids: 800+ Jokes!

Navigating Indieworld, with coauthor Julie A. Gerber

Marketing Indieworld, with coauthors Angela Hausman and Julie A. Gerber

Adult fiction under the pen name Brit Lunden:

Bulwark

The Knowing: A Bulwark Anthology